Richard Wagner

Die Walküre

Erster Tag aus der Trilogie: Der Ring des Nibelungen

Richard Wagner

Die Walküre
Erster Tag aus der Trilogie: Der Ring des Nibelungen

ISBN/EAN: 9783743340848

Hergestellt in Europa, USA, Kanada, Australien, Japan

Cover: Foto ©ninafisch / pixelio.de

Manufactured and distributed by brebook publishing software (www.brebook.com)

Richard Wagner

Die Walküre

DIE WALKÜRE.

ERSTER TAG AUS DER TRILOGIE:

DER RING DES NIBELUNGEN

VON

RICHARD WAGNER.

NEW YORK:
VERLAG VON CHARLES F. TRETBAR,
STEINWAY HALL.

CHARACTERS.	PERSONEN.
Siegmund.	Siegmund.
Hunding.	Hunding.
Wotan.	Wotan.
Sieglinda.	Sieglinde.
Brynhildr.	Brünnhilde.
Fricka.	Fricka.
Eight Valkyries.	Acht Walküren.

THE ARGUMENT.

ACT I. Siegmund, a warrior in flight, takes refuge one stormy evening in the house of Hunding, one of his enemies, whose wife, Sieglinda, arouses his interest and love. Hunding is bound by the laws of hospitality not to harm his guest till the morrow. In the night Sieglinda, having drugged her husband to sleep, elopes with the guest, who has plucked out a magic sword from a tree in which Wotan had plunged it, and the lovers at the same time discover themselves to be twin brother and sister, children of Wotan in the form of a hero, "Volsung."

ACT II. Fricka, the goddess of marriage, remonstrates with her truant husband, Wotan, on this outrage to her laws, and forces him to withdraw his protection from Siegmund and remove the power of his sword. A Valkyrie (corpse-chooser), Brynhildr, intended for his protection, is recalled and dispatched to tell him of his doom, but is so won upon by the hero's noble courage that she disobeys Wotan's command and strives to aid Siegmund in his combat with the pursuing Hunding. On this Wotan interposes in the fight himself, causing Siegmund's death. Then killing the unoffending Hunding in his rage, he turns his anger against the Valkyrie, who flies with Sieglinda.

ACT III. A band of Valkyries is assembled on a mountain top, on the way to Valhalla with the bodies of chosen warriors. To them flies Brynhildr for assistance, which they are disinclined to give. She resolves to save Sieglinda by sending her on, while she herself remains to bear the brunt of Wotan's anger. She tells Sieglinda that she shall be the mother of Siegfried, the greatest hero of the world, and that he shall restore the sword, of which she gives her the pieces. Wotan furiously arrives and, in spite of the intercession of the other Valkyries, deprives Brynhildr of her immortality and dooms her to lie in a charmed sleep for any man to wake and possess. All he concedes to her pleadings is to place a protecting wall of fire round her, that none but a hero may step through. Both know secretly that this deed is reserved for the unborn hero—Siegfried.

FIRST ACT.

Interior of a dwelling-place.

In the centre is the stem of a mighty ash-tree, the strong, upheaved roots of which spread far over the ground; the upper part of the tree is cut off from the rest by a wooden roof, which has holes to allow of the spreading limbs passing through; the umbrageous summit is supposed to overspread this roof. Round the tree-trunk, which forms the centre, a room is built; the walls are of roughly hewn logs, hung here and there with matting and woven hangings. R. in the foreground stands the hearth, the chimney of which goes sideways through the roof; behind the hearth is an inner room like a store-room, approached by mounting a few wooden steps; before this hangs a woven curtain, half thrown back. In the background an entrance-door with a smooth wooden latch. L. the door of an inner chamber, also led up to by steps; nearer down the stage, on the same side, a table with a broad wooden bench behind it, fixed to the wall and wooden stools in front.

A short orchestral prelude of a wild and stormy character forms the opening. At rise of the curtain *Siegmund* hastily opens the entrance door from without and enters; it is towards evening; a violent thunder storm is just subsiding.—*Siegmund* holds the latch in hand for a moment and scans the room; he seems exhausted by over-exertion, his dress and appearance indicate that he is in flight. Perceiving no one he closes the door behind him, strides to the hearth and there throws himself down, exhausted, on a rug of bearskin.

Siegmund.

Whose hearth this may be,
here I must rest me.

He sinks back and remains a while stretched out motionless. *Sieglinda* enters through the door of the inner chamber. Having heard a noise she has supposed it to be her husband returned home; her earnest look changes to surprise on finding a stranger reclining on the hearth.

Sieglinda
(still at back).

Whence came this man?
I must accost him.
(She quietly advances a few steps.)
Who entered here
and lies on the hearth?
(As *Siegmund* does not stir she approaches still closer and observes him.)
Tired is he
with the way's fatigue:
he seems insensible.—
Can he be sick?
(Bends closer to him.)
Still active his breathing,
though bound are his eyelids:
dauntless seems he, indeed,
though so drooping now.

Siegmund
(suddenly raising his head).

A draught! a draught!

ERSTER AUFZUG.

Das Innere eines Wohnraumes.

In der Mitte steht der Stamm einer mächtigen Esche, dessen stark erhabene Wurzeln sich weithin in den Erdboden verlieren; von seinem Wipfel ist der Baum durch ein gezimmertes Dach geschieden, welches so durchschnitten ist, dass der Stamm und die nach allen Seiten hin sich ausstreckenden Aeste durch genau entsprechende Oeffnungen hindurch gehen; von dem belaubten Wipfel wird angenommen, dass er sich über dieses Dach ausbreite. Um den Eschenstamm, als Mittelpunkt, ist nun ein Saal gezimmert; die Wände sind aus roh behauenem Holzwerk, hie und da mit geflochtenen und gewebten Decken behangen. Rechts im Vordergrund steht der Herd, dessen Rauchfang seitwärts zum Dache hinausführt; hinter dem Herde befindet sich ein innerer Raum, gleich einem Vorrathsspeicher, zu dem man auf einigen hölzernen Stufen hinaufsteigt; davor hängt, halb zurückgeschlagen, eine geflochtene Decke. Im Hintergrunde eine Eingangsthür mit schlichtem Holzriegel. Links die Thüre zu einem inneren Gemache, zu dem gleichfalls Stufen hinaufführen; weiter vorne auf derselben Seite ein Tisch mit einer breiten, an der Wand angezimmerten Bank dahinter, und hölzernen Schemeln davor.

Ein kurzes Orchester-Vorspiel von heftiger, stürmischer Bewegung leitet ein. Als der Vorhang aufgeht, öffnet *Siegmund* von aussen hastig die Eingangsthüre und tritt ein; es ist gegen Abend; starkes Gewitter, im Begriff sich zu legen. — *Siegmund* hält einen Augenblick den Riegel in der Hand, und überblickt den Wohnraum; er scheint von übermässiger Anstrengung erschöpft; sein Gewand und Aussehen zeigen, dass er sich auf der Flucht befinde. Da er Niemand gewahrt, schliesst er die Thüre hinter sich, schreitet auf den Herd zu und wirft sich dort ermattet auf eine Decke von Bärenfell.

Siegmund.

Wess' Herd dies auch sei,
hier muss ich rasten.

Er sinkt zurück und bleibt einige Zeit regungslos ausgestreckt. *Sieglinde* tritt aus der Thüre des inneren Gemaches. Dem vernommenen Geräusche nach glaubte sie ihren Mann heimgekehrt; ihre ernste Miene zeigt sich dann verwundert, als sie einen Fremden am Herde ausgestreckt findet.

Sieglinde
(noch im Hintergrunde).

Ein fremder Mann!
Ihn muss ich fragen.
(Sie tritt ruhig einige Schritte näher.)
Wer kam in's Haus
und liegt dort am Herd?
(Da *Siegmund* sich nicht regt, tritt sie noch etwas näher und betrachtet ihn.)
Müde liegt er
von Weges Müh'n:
schwanden die Sinne ihm?
wäre er siech? —
(Sie neigt sich näher zu ihm.)
Noch schwillt ihm der Athem;
das Auge nur schloss er: —
muthig dünkt mich der Mann,
sank er müd' auch hin.

Siegmund
(jäh das Haupt erhebend).

Ein Quell! ein Quell!

Sieglinda.

I'll draw thee water.

(She quickly takes a drinking horn, goes out of the house and returns with it full, then hands it to *Siegmund*.)

Lift but this
to thy lips dry and parching:—
water,—what thou dost wish.

(*Siegmund* drinks and hands her back the horn. After signing his thanks with his head his gaze rests with growing interest on her features.)

Siegmund.

Freshening liquid
here I have found;
my weary load
weigheth more light;
aroused are my wits,
my hopes arise,
the sense of sight is re-lit.—
Who is't restores me to life?

Sieglinda.

The house and the wife
of Hunding serve thee:
guestful greeting he'll give:
tarry but till he come.

Siegmund.

Weaponless am I:
a wounded guest.
Would thy goodman not wile me?

Sieglinda
(anxiously).

A wound! oh where is the hurt?

Siegmund
(shakes himself and springs up quickly to a sitting position).

'Tis well, trust me,—
unworthy of words;
I feel as erewhile
my sinews are firm.
Had but half so strong as mine arm
shield and spear been for havoc,
ne'er from foes had I fled; —
but they shivered my spear and shield.
The foe pursuing
pressed me so sore
and tempest-bruit
broke o'er my head;
but swifter than I from hunters,
speeds my heaviness hence:
sank on my lids dismal night,
but sunlight laughs on me now.

Sieglinde.

Erquickung schaff' ich.

(Sie nimmt schnell ein Trinkhorn, geht aus dem Hause und kommt mit dem gefüllten zurück, das sie *Siegmund* reicht.)

Labung biet' ich
dem lechzenden Gaumen:
Wasser, wie du gewollt!

Siegmund trinkt und reicht ihr das Horn zurück. Nachdem er ihr mit dem Kopfe Dank zugewinkt, haftet sein Blick länger mit steigender Theilnahme an ihren Mienen.

Siegmund.

Kühlende Labung
gab mir der Quell,
des Müden Last
machte er leicht;
erfrischt ist der Muth,
das Aug' erfreut
des Sehens selige Lust: —
wer ist's, der so mir es labt?

Sieglinde.

Dies Haus und dies Weib
sind Hundings Eigen;
gastlich gönn' er dir Rast:
harre bis heim er kehrt!

Siegmund.

Waffenlos bin ich:
dem wunden Gast
wird dein Gatte nicht wehren.

Sieglinde
(besorgt).

Die Wunden weise mir schnell!

Siegmund
(schüttelt sich und springt lebhaft vom Lager zu Sitz auf).

Gering sind sie,
der Rede nicht werth;
noch fügen des Leibes
Glieder sich fest.
Hätten halb so stark wie mein Arm
Schild und Speer mir gehalten,
nimmer floh' ich dem Feind; —
doch zerschellten mir Speer und Schild.
Der Feinde Meute
hetzte mich müd',
Gewitter-Brunst
brach meinen Leib;
doch schneller als ich der Meute,
schwand die Müdigkeit mir:
sank auf die Lider mir Nacht,
die Sonne lacht mir nun neu.

Sieglinda
(has filled a horn with mead and hands it him).

A freshening horn
of foaming mead
haply thou'llt not refuse?

Siegmund.
First wilt taste it thyself?

Sieglinda sips from the horn, and again proffers it; Siegmund takes a long draught; then he quickly takes the horn from his lips and returns it. They gaze silently at each other for some time with increasing emotion.

Siegmund
(with trembling voice).

An unfriended mortal tendest thou:—
Fortune ward
my woe from thee!
(He turns suddenly to go.)
Now strengthened am I
and well restored;
farther fareth my step.

Sieglinda
(turning quickly round).

Who doth follow, that thou must flee?

Siegmund
(enthralled by her voice, again returns: slowly and gloomily).

Ill fortune follows
fast on my footstep;
Ill fortune tracks me
wheree'er I tarry:
but from this may'st thou be free!
Forth shall my foot remove.
(He goes hastily to the door and lifts the latch.)

Sieglinda
(involuntarily and hastily calling to him).

Nay, bide thee here!
Thou'llt bring no ill-hap, methinks,
where ill-hap hath harboured long!

Siegmund
(deeply moved, remains motionless and searches Sieglinda's features: at length she casts down her eyes sadly and shyly. Long silence. Siegmund returns and sits down, leaning against the hearth).

"Woefull" have I been called:—
Hunding will I await here.

Sieglinda remains in troubled silence; then she starts, listens, and hears Hunding, who is leading his horse to the stable outside; she goes hastily to the door and opens it.

(Hunding, armed with shield and spear, enters and pauses at the threshold on perceiving Siegmund.

Sieglinde
(hat ein Horn mit Meth gefüllt und reicht es ihm).

Des seimigen Methes
süssen Trank
mög'st du mir nicht verschmäh'n.

Siegmund.
Schmecktest du mir ihn zu?

Sieglinde nippt am Horne, und reicht es ihm wieder; Siegmund thut einen langen Zug; dann setzt er schnell ab und reicht das Horn zurück. Beide blicken sich, mit wachsender Ergriffenheit, eine Zeit lang stumm an.

Siegmund
(mit bebender Stimme).

Einen Unseligen labtest du: —
Unheil wende
der Wunsch von dir!
(Er bricht schnell auf, um fortzugehen.)
Gerastet hab' ich
und süss geruh't:
weiter wend' ich den Schritt.

Sieglinde
(lebhaft sich umwendend).

Wer verfolgt dich, dass du schon flieh'st?

Siegmund
(von ihrem Rufe gefesselt, wendet sich wieder: langsam und düster).

Misswende folgt mir
wohin ich fliehe;
Misswende naht mir
wo ich mich neige:
dir Frau doch bleibe sie fern!
Fort wend' ich Fuss und Blick.
(Er schreitet schnell bis zur Thüre, und hebt den Riegel.)

Sieglinde
(in heftigem Selbstvergessen im nachrufend).

So bleibe hier!
Nicht bringst du Unheil dahin,
wo Unheil im Hause wohnt!

Siegmund
(bleibt tief erschüttert stehen, und forscht in Sieglinde's Mienen: diese schlägt endlich verschämt und traurig die Augen nieder. Langes Schweigen. Siegmund kehrt zurück, und lässt sich, an den Herd gelehnt, nieder).

Wehwalt hiess ich mich selbst: —
Hunding will ich erwarten.

Sieglinde verharrt in betretenem Schweigen; dann fährt sie auf, lauscht, und hört Hunding, der sein Ross aussen zu Stall führt; sie geht hastig zur Thüre und öffnet.

(Hunding, gewaffnet mit Schild und Speer, tritt ein, und hält unter der Thüre, als er Siegmund gewahrt.)

Sieglinda
(encountering the look of stern enquiry cast on her by *Hunding*).
He—this guest,
sank on our hearth,
rest seeking to gain.

Hunding.
His need's supplied?

Sieglinda.
I gave him nourishment,
gladly harboured him.

Siegmund
(firmly and quietly watching *Hunding*).
Aid and rest
I have had:
choose you to chide the woman?

Hunding.
Holy is my hearth:—
haven find in my house!
(To *Sieglinda*, as he doffs his weapons and gives them over to her.)
Haste our suppers to serve!
Sieglinda hangs the weapons on the tree, fetches provisions from the store-room and lays the table for supper.

Hunding
(scanning sharply and with surprise *Siegmund's* features, which he compares with those of his wife—aside):
How like is their seeming!
That look of a snake
likewise gleams in his glances.
(He hides his surprise, and turns unconcernedly to *Siegmund*.)
Sure from far
thy way was shaped?
no horse had he
who halted here:
what rugged path
has wrought thee such pain?

Siegmund.
Through thorn and thicket,
forest and fen,
I was pursued
by storm and foes:
I trow not the way that I took.
Whither I've wandered
wist I no better:
tidings I'd willingly learn.

Hunding
(at the table and signing *Siegmund* to a seat).
This resting roof,
this harbouring house,
Hunding holds for wealth;

Sieglinde
(dem ernst fragenden Blicke, den *Hunding* auf sie richtet, entgegnend).
Müd' am Herd
fand ich den Mann:
Noth führt' ihn in's Haus.

Hunding.
Du labtest ihn?

Sieglinde.
Den Gaumen letzt' ich ihm,
gastlich sorgt' ich sein'.

Siegmund
(der fest und ruhig *Hunding* beobachtet).
Dach und Trank
dank ich ihr:
willst du dein Weib drum schelten?

Hunding.
Heilig ist mein Herd:—
heilig sei dir mein Haus!
(Zu *Sieglinde*, indem er die Waffen ablegt und ihr übergibt.)
Rüst' uns Männern das Mahl!
Sieglinde hängt die Waffen am Eschenstamme auf, holt Speise und Trank aus dem Speicher und rüstet auf dem Tische das Nachtmahl.

Hunding
(misst scharf und verwundert *Siegmund's* Züge, die er mit denen seiner Frau vergleicht; für sich):
Wie gleicht er dem Weibe!
Der gleissende Wurm
glänzt auch ihm aus dem Auge.
(Er birgt sein Befremden u. wendet sich unbefangen zu *Siegmund*.)
Weit her, traun!
kamst du des Weg's;
ein Ross nicht ritt,
der Rast hier fand:
welch' schlimme Pfade
schufen dir Pein?

Siegmund.
Durch Wald und Wiese,
Haide und Hain,
jagte mich Sturm
und starke Noth:
nicht kenn' ich den Weg, den ich kam.
Wohin ich irrte
weiss ich noch minder:
Kunde gewänn' ich dess' gern.

Hunding
(am Tische und *Siegmund* den Sitz bietend).
Dess' Dach dich deckt,
dess' Haus dich hegt,
Hunding heisst der Wirth;

wendest thou hence
to the west thy way,
in homesteads rich
hordes of my kinsmen
uphold the honour of Hunding.
Grant the favour, my guest,
that thy name may not be unknown.

Siegmund, who has seated himself at table, gazes thoughtfully before him. *Sieglinda* has placed herself beside *Hunding*, opposite to *Siegmund*, and fixes her eyes on the latter with strange interest and expectancy.

Hunding
(observing them both).

Care or trouble
hast to disclose,
my wife would gladly listen:
See, how greedily she waits!

Sieglinda
(unembarrassed and with interest).

Guest, who thou art
I would glean.

Siegmund
(looks up, gazes into her eyes and begins earnestly).

"Peaceful" may I not call me;
"Joyful" would I had been!
But "Woeful" must be my title.
Wolfing, he was my father;
as twins entered the world
my tender sister and I.
Full soon I lost
mother and maid;
the parent fond
and the playfellow fair:
nay, they have scarcely been known.—
Warlike and strong was Wolfing,
and foes he won not a few.
Through forest fared we
in forage together;
when home from the hunt
one even we hied
the Wolfing's nest lay waste.
To cinders burnt
the building so strong,
to stumps the oak-tree's
blossoming stem,
and slaughtered the mother
motionless lay,
no signs of my sister
the cinders shewed:
this shameful deed we knew
the Neidings had done, for sure.
Then friendless fled
my father with me;

wendest von hier du
nach West den Schritt,
in Höfen reich
hausen dort Sippen,
die Hunding's Ehre behüten.
Gönnt mir Ehre mein Gast,
wird sein Name nun mir genannt.

Siegmund, der sich am Tisch niedergesetzt, blickt nachdenklich vor sich hin. *Sieglinde* hat sich neben *Hunding*, *Siegmund* gegenüber, gesetzt, und heftet mit auffallender Theilnahme und Spannung ihr Auge auf diesen.

Hunding
(der beide beobachtet).

Trägst du Sorge,
mir zu vertrau'n,
der Frau hier gieb doch Kunde:
sieh', wie sie gierig dich frägt!

Sieglinde
(unbefangen und theilnahmvoll).

Gast, wer du bist,
wüsst' ich gern.

Siegmund
(blickt auf, sieht ihr in das Auge, und beginnt ernst).

Friedmund darf ich nicht heissen;
Frohwalt möcht ich wohl sein:
doch Wehwalt muss ich mich nennen.
Wolfe, der war mein Vater;
zu zwei kam ich zur Welt,
eine Zwillingsschwester und ich.
Früh schwanden mir
Mutter und Maid;
die mich gebar,
und die mit mir sie barg,
kaum hab' ich je sie gekannt. —
Wehrlich und stark war Wolfe;
der Feinde wuchsen ihm viel.
Zum Jagen zog
mit dem Jungen der Alte;
von Hetze und Harst
einst kehrten sie heim:
da lag das Wolfsnest leer;
zu Schutt gebrannt
der prangende Saal,
zum Stumpf der Eiche
blühender Stamm;
erschlagen der Mutter
muthiger Leib,
verschwunden in Gluthen
der Schwester Spur:
uns schuf die herbe Noth
der Neidinge harte Schaar.
Geächtet floh
der Alte mit mir;

lapsed my youth
while living for years
with Wolfing in woodlands wild:
onsets yet
against us were aimed,
but ever warded
the Wolves themselves.
(turning to *Hunding*.)
A Wolfing now relates this,
and as Wolfing I am well known.

Hunding.

Wild and unwonted stories
tell'st thou, intrepid guest.
Woeful—the Wolfing,
I've heard of that warrior pair
full oft unholy stories,
I myself neither
have known till now.

Sieglinda.

Yet, stranger, tell us further:
where stays thy father now?

Siegmund.

An onslaught mighty of aim
ordered the Neidings on us;
but many foemen
fell by the Wolfings,
their flight through the wood
others did wing;
like chaff we chased them afar.
I strayed from my father by chance:
he, my chief, was wanting,
though wearily watched for·
but alone a wolf-skin
lay in the wood,
toss'd tenantless there:
my father found I not.—
After this shunned were the woods;
I sheltered with heroes and women.
But far and near,
wheree'er I fared,
if for a friend
or fair I wished
I could not win what I asked for:
ill luck lay on me.
When recking I was right
wrong to others I wrought;
and things ill, as I thought,
others hotly upheld.
I fell in feud
wherever I fared;
strife came
wherever I strayed;

lange Jahre
lebte der Junge
mit Wolfe im wilden Wald:
manche Jagd
ward auf sie gemacht;
doch muthig wehrte
das Wolfspaar sich.
(Zu *Hunding* gewendet.)
Ein Wölfing kündet dir das,
den als Wölfing mancher wohl kennt.

Hunding.

Wunder und wilde Märe
kündest du, kühner Gast,
Wehwalt — der Wölfing!
Mich dünkt, von dem wehrlichen Paar
vernahm ich dunkle Sage,
kannt' ich auch Wolfe
und Wölfing nicht.

Sieglinde.

Doch weiter künde, Fremder:
wo weilt dein Vater jetzt?

Siegmund.

Ein starkes Jagen auf uns
stellten die Neidinge an:
der Jäger viele
fielen den Wölfen,
in Flucht durch den Wald
trieb sie das Wild:
wie Spreu zerstob uns der Feind.
Doch ward ich vom Vater versprengt:
seine Spur verlor ich,
je länger ich forschte;
eines Wolfes Fell
nur traf ich im Forst:
leer lag das vor mir,
den Vater fand ich nicht. —
Aus dem Wald trieb es mich fort;
mich drängt' es zu Männern und Frauen:
wie viel ich traf,
wo ich sie fand,
ob ich um Freund,
um Frauen warb, —
immer doch war ich geächtet,
Unheil lag auf mir.
Was rechtes je ich rieth,
andern dünkte es arg;
was schlimm immer mir schien,
andre gaben ihm Gunst.
In Fehde fiel ich,
wo ich mich fand;
Zorn traf mich
wohin ich zog;

did I seek pleasure
pain but appeared:—
they call we then "Woeful" rightly;
unwitting, woe I must wreak.

Hunding.

Sure the Norn who knitted thy fate
had nought of love for thee.
Neither hails thee the man
who now the host must play.

Sieglinda.

Foolish 'twere fear to hold
of one o'erta'en by defeat! —
Tell us now, guest,
in what attack
of late thy weapons were lost?

Siegmund
(with increasing animation).

For succour a maid
loudly besought,
whom chiding kin
would have chained and wed
to a churl whom the child did not choose.
Swift to her aid
urged I my way;
the heartless crew
crushing in fight:
before my force they sank.
I slew the brethren relentless;
their bodies the sister embraced,
her panic yielded to pain.
In floods of wildest tears
she wailed the fiat of fate:
for her brothers inhuman murder
.oudly to heaven she moaned. —
Then the slain men's servants
swooped to the spot;
crowding on me
cried they for punishment,
pouring around me
panted the rabble;
yet from the mourned
moved not the maid:
my shield and spear
sheltered her long,
till spear and shield
were hewn from my hands.
Weak and weaponless standing,
soon I saw her expire:
still menaced the furious mob, —
but the maiden moved no more.

gehrt' ich nach Wonne,
weckt' ich nur Weh': —
drum musst' ich mich Wehwalt nennen;
des Wehes waltet' ich nur.

Hunding.

Die so leidig Loos dir beschied,
nicht liebte dich die Norn:
froh nicht grüsst dich der Mann,
dem fremd als Gast du nah'st.

Sieglinde.

Feige nur fürchten den,
der waffenlos einsam fährt! —
Künde noch, Gast,
wie du im Kampf
zuletzt die Waffe verlor'st!

Siegmund.
(immer lebhafter).

Ein trauriges Kind
rief mich zum Trutz:
vermählen wollte
der Magen Sippe
dem Mann ohne Minne die Maid.
Wider den Zwang
zog ich zum Schutz;
der Dränger Tross
traf ich im Kampf:
dem Sieger sank der Feind.
Erschlagen lagen die Brüder:
die Leichen umschlang da die Maid;
den Grimm verjagt' ihr der Gram.
Mit wilder Thränen Fluth
betroff sie weinend die Wal:
um des Mordes der eig'nen Brüder
klagte die unsel'ge Braut. —
Der Erschlag'nen Sippen
stürmten daher;
übermächtig
ächzten nach Rache sie,
rings um die Stätte
ragten mir Feinde.
Doch von der Wal
wich nicht die Maid:
mit Schild und Speer
schirmt' ich sie lang',
bis Speer und Schild
im Harst mir zerhau'n.
Wund und waffenlos stand ich —
sterben sah ich die Maid:
mich hetzte das wüthende Heer —
auf den Leichen lag sie todt.

THE VALKYRIE.

(With a glance of painful ardour towards *Sieglinda*.)
So, mistress, knowest thou now
why I may name me not "Joyful."
(He rises and walks over to the hearth. *Sieglinde* casts down her eyes, pale and deeply moved.)

Hunding
(darkly).

I trow, a truculent race!
Our holiest laws
ye lightly hold;
the hatred of all ye have earned.
They sought but now my assistance
vengeance to render
for vassals' blood.
They sent too late;
returning now home
the flying foe himself
upon my hearth do I see. —
My house holds thee,
Wolfing, from harm,
for this night know thou art safe:
but arms redoutable
don with the morning;
at dawn of day shalt thou fall,
my fellows' cause to requite.
(To *Sieglinda*, who with anxious gestures steps between the two men.)
Forth from the hall!
Hence without pause!
Prepare my evening draught,
and wait for me within.

Sieglinda thoughtfully takes a drinking horn from the table, goes to a cupboard from which she takes spices, and turns towards the side chamber: on the uppermost step by the door she again turns and fixes on *Siegmund*—who in suppressed anger stands quietly by the hearth only gazing at her—a long wistful look, with which at last she directs his attention meaningly and earnestly to a spot in the ash-tree. *Hunding*, perceiving her delay, drives her away with a commanding gesture, whereupon she disappears through the door with the drinking horn and the light.

Hunding
(taking his weapons from the tree).

Beware these weapons of mine! —
Thou, Wolfing, diest to-morrow:
my words hearken to —
heed thyself well!
(He goes into the chamber with the arms.)

Siegmund
(alone).

It has now become quite night: the room is only lit by a dull fire on the hearth. *Siegmund* sinks down on the bench by the fire, and reflects for some time in silent perturbation.

A sword once promised my father
to furnish in pressing need. —
Weaponless fall'n,
into foemen's lair,

(Mit einem Blicke voll schmerzlichen Feuers auf *Sieglinde*.)
Nun weisst du, fragende Frau,
Warum ich — Friedmund nicht heisse!
(Er steht auf und schreitet auf den Herd zu. *Sieglinde* blickt erbleichend und tief erschüttert zu Boden.)

Hunding
(sehr finster).

Ich weiss ein wildes Geschlecht,
nicht heilig ist ihm
was andren hehr:
verhasst ist es Allen und mir.
Zur Rache ward ich gerufen,
Sühne zu nehmen
für Sippen-Blut:
zu spät kam ich,
und kehre nun heim
des flücht'gen Frevlers Spur
im eig'nen Haus zu erspäh'n. —
Mein Haus hütet,
Wölfing, dich heut';
für die Nacht nahm ich dich auf:
mit starker Waffe
doch wehre dich morgen;
zum Kampfe kies' ich den Tag:
für Todte zahlst du mir Zoll.
(Zu *Sieglinde*, die sich mit besorgter Gebärde zwischen die beiden Männer stellt.)
Fort aus dem Saal!
Säume hier nicht!
Den Nachttrunk rüste mir drin,
und harre mein' zur Ruh'.

Sieglinde nimmt sinnend ein Trinkhorn vom Tisch, geht zu einem Schrein, aus dem sie Würze nimmt, und wendet sich nach dem Seitengemache: auf der obersten Stufe bei der Thüre angelangt, wendet sie sich noch einmal um, und richtet auf *Siegmund*—der mit verhaltenem Grimme ruhig am Herde steht, und einzig sie im Auge behält — einen langen, sehnsüchtigen Blick, mit welchem sie ihn endlich auf eine Stelle im Eschenstamme bedeutungsvoll auffordernd hinweist. *Hunding*, der ihr Zögern bemerkt, treibt sie dann mit einem gebietenden Winke fort, worauf sie mit dem Trinkhorn und der Leuchte durch die Thüre verschwindet.

Hunding
(nimmt seine Waffen vom Baume).

Mit Waffen wahrt sich der Mann. —
Dich Wölfing treff' ich morgen:
mein Wort hörtest du —
hüte dich wohl!
(Er geht mit den Waffen in das Gemach ab.)

Siegmund
(allein).

Es ist vollständig Nacht geworden; der Saal ist nur noch von einem matten Feuer im Herde erhellt. *Siegmund* lässt sich, nah beim Feuer, auf dem Lager nieder, und brütet in grosser Aufregung eine Zeit lang schweigend vor sich hin.

Ein Schwert verhiess mir der Vater,
ich fänd' es in höchster Noth. —
Waffenlos fiel ich
in Feindes Haus:

as a hostage doomed
here do I lie. —
A wife I saw,
wondrously fair;
and strange emotion
stirred my frame:—
to her do my longings stray,
who hath lured my soul toward love.—
In servance holds her this man,
who mocks my swordless hand.—
Volsung! Volsung!
Where is thy sword?
thy sturdy sword,
that in strife should serve me?
Breaks madly forth from my breast
the frenzy my heart would hide?

The fire falls together; from the up-springing glow a bright ray strikes on that spot of the ash-tree stem indicated by Sieglinda's look, and where a buried sword hilt is now plainly perceptible.

What gleam from out
the glow doth shoot?
What a star breaks
from the ash-tree's stem?
Before mine eyes
a lightning doth flash;
lo, it laughs in my face!—
How the sunny glow
doth glad my soul!
Is it the look
the lovely one threw,
which yet lingers
alluringly there,
though from the hall she hied?

(Here the fire fades out gradually.)

Deepening shadow
shrouded mine eyes;
but on me her glance
gloriously shone:
wondrous the warmth that it shed.
Gleamed in grandeur
the golden sun,
his glittering halo
encircled my head
till he retired to rest.
Yet once more ere it left
kindled evening's soft light;
e'en the aged ash-tree's limbs
he gladdened with golden glow.
The flush is fading —
the light sinks low —
deepening shadow
shroudeth my eyelids:
deep in my heart lies hid
a faint but still smouldering fire!

The fire has quite gone out: complete darkness.—The side door opens gently: Sieglinda in a white robe enters and approaches Siegmund.

seiner Rache Pfand
rast' ich hier: —
ein Weib sah' ich,
wonnig und hehr;
entzückendes Bangen
zehret mein Herz:—
zu der mich nun Sehnsucht zieht,
die mit süssem Zauber mich sehrt —
im Zwange hält sie der Mann,
der mich — Wehrlosen höhnt. —
Wälse! Wälse!
Wo ist dein Schwert?
Das starke Schwert,
das im Sturm ich schwänge,
bricht mir hervor aus der Brust
was wüthend das Herz noch hegt?

Das Feuer bricht zusammen; es fällt aus der aufsprühenden Gluth ein greller Schein auf die Stelle des Eschenstammes, welche Sieglinde's Blick bezeichnet hatte, und an der man jetzt deutlich einen Schwertgriff haften sieht.

Was gleisst dort hell
im Glimmerschein?
Welch' ein Strahl bricht
aus der Esche Stamm? —
Des Blinden Auge
leuchtet ein Blitz:
lustig lacht da der Blick. —
Wie der Schein so hehr
das Herz mir sengt!
Ist es der Blick
der blühenden Frau,
den dort haftend
sie hinter sich liess,
als aus dem Saal sie schied?

(Von hier an verglimmt das Herdfeuer allmälig.)

Nächtiges Dunkel
deckte mein Aug';
ihres Blickes Strahl
streifte mich da:
Wärme gewann ich und Tag.
Selig schien mir
der Sonne Licht,
den Scheitel umgliss mir
ihr wonniger Glanz —
bis hinter Bergen sie sank.
Noch einmal, da sie schied,
traf mich Abends ihr Schein
selbst der alten Esche Stamm
erglänzte in gold'ner Gluth:
da bleicht die Blüthe —
das Licht verlischt —
nächt'ges Dunkel
deckt mir das Auge:
tief in des Busens Berge
glimmt nur noch lichtlose Gluth!

Das Feuer ist gänzlich verloschen: volle Nacht. — Das Seitengemach öffnet sich leise: Sieglinde, in weissem Gewande, tritt heraus, und schreitet auf Siegmund zu.

Sieglinda.
Sleep'st thou, guest?

Siegmund
(springing up with joyful surprise)
Who steals toward?

Sieglinda
(with secrecy and haste).
See me—hear what I say!—
In deepest sleep lies Hunding;
I mingled a drug with his drink.
Haste from this house without fear.

Siegmund
(ardently interrupting her).
Fear drivest thou hence!

Sieglinda.
To a goodly weapon I'll guide thee—
a glorious prize to gain!
As highest hero
then I might hail thee;
the strongest alone
bears off that steel.
Oh ponder well what I repeat thee!—
His people Hunding
had in this hall
with wassail his wedding to honour:
he wedded a maid
whom ne'er he wooed;
ravishers wrought her this woe.
Misery filled me
while all were merry:
when sudden marked I a man—
in garments gray, and full old;
low hung was his hat,
and one of his eyes 'twas over;
but the other's flash
awe forced on all men;
ev'ry heart felt
its haughty power;
howbeit I
gleaned from that look
sweet solace and pain,
gladness and grief in one.
On me smiling,
he scowled at the others,
as a sword he solemnly swung;
then struck it deep
in the ashtree's stem;
with a blow buried it there.
To none should the prize be fated
but who could pluck it forth.

Sieglinde.
Schläfst du, Gast?

Siegmund
(freudig überrascht aufspringend).
Wer schleicht daher?

Sieglinde
(mit geheimnissvoller Hast).
Ich bin's: höre mich an!—
In tiefem Schlaf liegt Hunding;
ich würzt' ihm betäubenden Trank
Nütze die Nacht dir zum Heil!

Siegmund
(hitzig unterbrechend).
Heil macht mich dein Nah'n!

Sieglinde.
Eine Waffe lass' mich dir weisen —
O wenn du sie gewänn'st!
Den hehr'sten Helden
dürft' ich dich heissen;
dem Stärk'sten allein
ward sie bestimmt.
O merke was ich dir melde!—
Der Männer Sippe
sass hier im Saal,
von Hunding zur Hochzeit geladen:
er frei'te ein Weib,
das ungefragt
Schächer ihm schenkten zur Frau.
Traurig sass ich
während sie tranken:
ein Fremder trat da herein —
ein Greis in grauem Gewand;
tief hing ihm der Hut,
der deckt' ihm der Augen eines;
doch des andren Strahl,
Angst schuf er allen,
traf die Männer
sein mächt'ges Dräu'n:
mir allein
weckte das Auge
süss sehnenden Harm,
Thränen und Trost zugleich.
Auf mich blickt' er,
und blitzte auf Jene,
als ein Schwert in Händen er schwang;
das stiess er nun
in der Esche Stamm,
bis zum Heft haftet' es drin: —
dem sollte der Stahl geziemen,
der aus dem Stamm' es zög'.

Then valiant heroes
bestirred them all vainly,
the wondrous steel none might win.
Warriors strayed here
and warriors wended,
the stoutest laboured and strove —
but they loosed it not from the stem:
yet bides the sword in its sheath. —
Ah! well I wist who 'twas
who so gravely me did greet:
his name too
I know well
for whom that hilt is withheld.
Oh found I in need
but now that friend!
came he from far
my distress to find,
whate'er I had suffered
in anguish of soul,
howe'er I had pined
in penance and pain,
sweet consolation
surely would follow!
Then all losses
should I have retrieved,
what erst I bewailed
well might be won me,
found I this help-giving friend,
and folded him in these arms.

Siegmund
(embracing her with fiery ardour).

Thou'rt now, mistress fair,
held by that friend,
who weapon and wife doth claim!
Warm in this heart
hidden doth lie
the thought that links me to thee.
Whate'er I have sought,
I see here in thee;
in thee liveth
whate'er I have lacked!
Wept thou for wrongs,
I writhed too in woe;
I was degraded,
thou also disgraced;
loudly revenge's
voice now delights me!
I laugh out
with triumph elate,
holding thee, highest and fairest —
feeling the beat of thy heart.

Sieglinda
(starts in alarm and tears herself loose).

Ha! who pass'd? who entered here?

Der Männer Alle,
so kühn sie sich müh'ten,
die Wehr sich keiner gewann;
Gäste kamen
und Gäste gingen,
die stärk'sten zogen am Stahl —
keinen Zoll entwich er dem Stamm:
dort haftet schweigend das Schwert. —
Da wusst' ich, wer der war,
der mich Gramvolle gegrüsst:
ich weiss auch
wem allein
im Stamm das Schwert er bestimmt.
O fänd' ich ihn heut'
und hier, den Freund;
käm' er aus Fremden
zur ärmsten Frau:
was je ich gelitten
in grimmigem Leid,
was je mich geschmerzt
in Schand' und Schmach, —
süsseste Rache
sühnte dann Alles!
Erjagt hätt' ich
was je ich verlor,
was je ich beweint
wär' mir gewonnen —
fänd' ich den heiligen Freund,
umfing' den Helden mein Arm!

Siegmund
(umfasst sie mit feuriger Gluth).

Dich selige Frau
hält nun der Freund,
dem Waffe und Weib bestimmt!
Heiss in der Brust
brennt mir der Eid,
der mich dir Edlen vermählt.
Was je ich ersehnt,
ersah' ich in dir;
in dir fand ich,
was je mir gefehlt!
Littest du Schmach,
und schmerzte mich Leid;
war ich geächtet,
und warst du entehrt;
freudige Rache
ruft nun den Frohen!
Auf lach' ich
in heiliger Lust,
halt' ich dich Hehre umfangen,
fühl' ich dein schlagendes Herz!

Sieglinde
(fährt erschrocken zusammen und reisst sich los).

Ha, wer ging? wer kam herein?

THE VALKYRIE.

The door at back has sprung open and remains wide: outside is a lovely Spring night; the full-moon shines in, throwing its bright light on the pair, who can now suddenly and plainly behold each other.

Siegmund
(in soft ecstasy).

No one pass'd —
but one draws nigh:
lo now, where Spring
spreads o'er the land!

(He draws her to him with tender impetuosity on the bench.)

Winter storms have waned
'neath the winsome moon,
in mild ascendance
smileth the Spring;
and, swayed by Zephyrs
soft and soothing,
weaving wonders
lo! he wends.
Through wood and broadland
wafts his breathing,
widely beam
his eyes with bliss.
In songs of birds resounds
his silvery voice,
pleasant odours
pours he forth;
from his living blood out-burst
the loveliest blossoms;
verdant sprays
up-spring at his voice.
With softly wielded sceptre
sways he the world;
Winter and storm wane
as his strength awakes: —
Oh well may his hardy striving
the stubborn hinges be riving,
which, heavy and stiff,
once—held us from him! —
Towards his sister
swiftly he flieth;
longing Love Spring allures.
Within our bosoms
buried she slept;
now leaps she forth to the light.
The bride and the sister
is freed by the brother;
lie prone the walls
that held them apart;
hail each other
the happy pair:
now Spring at last holds his Love.

Sieglinda.

Thou art the Spring,
for thee have I sighed
'neath the frost-fettered winter's frown.

Die hintere Thüre ist aufgesprungen und bleibt weit geöffnet: aussen herrliche Frühlingsnacht; der Vollmond leuchtet herein und wirft sein helles Licht auf das Paar, das so sich plötzlich in voller Deutlichkeit wahrnehmen kann.

Siegmund
(in leiser Entzückung).

Keiner ging —
doch Einer kam:
siehe, der Lenz
lacht in den Saal!

(Er zieht sie mit sanftem Ungestüm zu sich auf das Lager.)

Winterstürme wichen
dem Wonnemond,
in mildem Lichte
leuchtet der Lenz;
auf lauen Lüften
lind und lieblich,
Wunder webend
er sich wiegt;
über Wald und Auen
went sein Athem,
weit geöffnet
lacht sein Aug'.
Aus sel'ger Vöglein Sange
süss er tönt,
holdeste Düfte
haucht er aus;
seinem warmen Blut entblühen
wonnige Blumen.
Keim und Spross
entspriesst seiner Kraft.
Mit zarter Waffen Zier
bezwingt er die Welt.
Winter und Sturm wichen
der starken Wehr: —
wohl musste den tapfren Streichen
die strenge Thüre auch weichen,
die trotzig und starr
uns — trennte von ihm. —
Zu seiner Schwester
schwang er sich her;
die Liebe lockte den Lenz;
in uns'rem Busen
barg sie sich tief:
nun lacht sie selig dem Licht.
Die bräutliche Schwester
befreite der Bruder;
zertrümmert liegt
was sie getrennt;
jauchzend grüsst sich
das junge Paar:
vereint sind Liebe und Lenz!

Sieglinde.

Du bist der Lenz,
nach dem ich verlangte
in frostigen Winter's Frist;

Tow'rd thee leapt my heart
with heavenly thrill
when thy radiant glance on me rested.—
Foreign seemed all until now,
friendless I and forsaken;
I counted strange and unknown
each and all that came near.
But thee, now, I
thoroughly knew;
when these eyes fell on thee
wert thou mine own one.
What my heart long had held,
what was hid,
clear as the day
dawned on my eyes,
the dulcet refrain
fell on my ear,
when in winter's frosty wildness
a friend first awaited me.

(She hangs in rapture on his neck and gazes closely into his face.)

Siegmund.

O wondrous vision!
woman divine!

Sieglinda
(close to his eyes).

Let me closer
embracing clasp thee,
that I may look on
the angel light
which from thine eyes
in ardour breaks,
and so sweetly swayeth my sense!

Siegmund.

The Spring's fair moon
streams on thy head,
hanging a wreath
o'er thy rippling hair:
what 'twas bewitched me
well now I feel —
I feast in fervour mine eyes.

Sieglinda
(pushing back the locks from his brow, and gazing at him with wonder).

How fair and broad
thy open brow!
the varying veins
in thy temples I trace.
I tremble with emotion,
resting entranced: —
a memory masters my spirit: —
though but to-day met we first,
I deem not strange thy face!

dich grüsste mein Herz
mit heil'gem Grau'n,
als dein Blick zuerst mir erblühte. —
Fremdes nur sah ich von je,
freundlos war mir das Nahe;
als hätt' ich nie es gekannt
war was immer mir kam.
Doch dich kannt' ich
deutlich und klar:
als mein Auge dich sah,
warst du mein Eigen:
was im Busen ich barg,
was ich bin,
hell wie der Tag
taucht' es mir auf,
wie tönender Schall
schlug's an mein Ohr,
als in frostig öder Fremde
zuerst den Freund ich ersah.

(Sie hängt sich entzückt an seinen Hals, und blickt ihm nahe in's Gesicht).

Siegmund.

O süsseste Wonne!
seligstes Weib!

Sieglinde
(dicht an seinen Augen).

Lass in Nähe
zu dir mich neigen,
dass deutlich ich schaue
den hehren Schein,
der dir aus Augen
und Antlitz bricht,
und so süss die Sinne mir zwingt!

Siegmund.

Im Lenzesmond
leuchtest du hell;
hehr umwebt dich
das Wellenhaar;
was mich berückt
errath' ich nun leicht —
denn wonnig weidet mein Blick.

Sieglinde
(schlägt ihm die Locken von der Stirn zurück, und betrachtet ihn staunend).

Wie dir die Stirn
so offen steht,
in den Schläfen der Adern
Geäst sich schlingt!
Mir zagt's vor der Wonne,
die mich entzückt —
ein Wunder will mich gemahnen: —
den heut' zuerst ich erschaut,
mein Auge sah dich schon!

Siegmund.
Such fairy dreams
my fancy filled:
thy form I viewed
in visions of bliss!

Sieglinda.
In streams my semblance
I often saw—
again it floateth before me;
as erst from the river it rose,
mildly 'tis mirrored in thee.

Siegmund.
Thine was the picture
that to me appeared.

Sieglinda.
(suddenly turning away her face).
O hush! let me
unhindered listen: —
thy voice seems to peal
out from the past — —
yet hold! more lately I heard it;
when through the waving woods
the echo came of my own.

Siegmund.
O loveliest lute
to which I now listen!

Sieglinda
(again quickly searching his features).
Well I know the light
that lurks in thine eyes: —
so once the strange guest
greeting bestowed,
when he solemnly soothed my grief.
In that fiery glance
my father I felt—
his name I had fain uttered fondly—
(She pauses, then resumes softly.)
"Woefull" calls thee the word?

Siegmund.
Ne'er call me so
since thou art mine:
I rest now in highest rapture.

Sieglinda.
Nor "Joyful" may be
justly thy title?

Siegmund.
Name me thyself
as thou judgest my nature:
I'll take my title from thee.

Siegmund.
Ein Minnetraum
gemahnt auch mich:
in heissem Sehnen
sah ich dich schon!

Sieglinde.
Im Bach erblickt' ich
mein eigen Bild —
und jetzt gewahr' ich es wieder:
wie einst dem Teich es enttaucht,
bietest mein Bild mir nun du!

Siegmund.
Du bist das Bild —
das ich in mir barg.

Sieglinde
(den Blick schnell abwendend).
O still! lass mich
der Stimme lauschen: —
mich dünkt, ihren Klang
hört' ich als Kind — —
doch nein! ich hörte sie neulich,
als meiner Stimme Schall
mir wiederhallte der Wald.

Siegmund
O lieblichste Laute,
denen ich lausche!

Sieglinde
(schnell ihm wieder in's Auge spähend).
Deines Auges Gluth
erglänzte mir schon: —
so blickte der Greis
grüssend auf mich,
als der Traurigen Trost er gab.
An dem kühnen Blick
erkannt' ihn sein Kind —
schon wollt' ich bei'm Namen ihn nennen —
(Sie hält inne, und fährt dann leise fort.)
Wehwalt heiss'st du fürwahr?

Siegmund.
Nicht heiss' ich so
seit du mich liebst:
nun walt' ich der hehrsten Wonnen!

Sieglinde.
Und Friedmund darfst du
froh dich nicht nennen?

Siegmund.
Heisse mich du
wie du liebst dass ich heisse:
den Namen nehm' ich von dir!

Sieglinda.
Then truly was Wolfing thy father?

Siegmund.
A wolf he to fearful foxes!
But he whose eye
on thee is beaming
as flashes, oh fair one! thine own,
avers—Volsung his name.

Sieglinda
(transported.)
Was Volsung thy father—
art thou too a Volsung?
Struck he for thee
yon sword in the stem?
So let me then name thee
as I do love thee:
Siegmund—
so be thou called!

Siegmund
(springing up to the tree and grasping the sword-hilt).
Siegmund hight I
and Siegmund am I:
a witness this sword;
unwav'ring I seize it!
Volsung assured me
in sorest need
mine it should be:
I'll make it so!
Holy affection,
highest need—
passionate longing,
pressingest need,
brightly flame in my breast,
drive to deeds and death.—
Needful! Needful!—
I name so this sword—
Needful! Needful!
notable steel!
prove me thy sharpness,
shew me thy point:
leap forth from thy sheath at my call!
(With a mighty effort he plucks the sword out of the tree and holds it up before the enraptured and wonder-stricken *Sieglinda*.)
Siegmund the Volsung
stands revealed!
for bride-gift
he brings thee this sword;
and fearless woos
a wife sweet and fair;
from foeman's house
he flies with his bride.
Far from hence
follow his steps,

Sieglinde.
Doch nanntest du Wolfe den Vater?

Siegmund.
Ein Wolf war er feigen Füchsen!
Doch dem so stolz
strahlte das Auge,
wie, Herrliche, hehr dir es strahlt,
der war — Wälse genannt.

Sieglinde
(ausser sich).
War Wälse dein Vater,
und bist du ein Wälsung,
stiess er für dich
sein Schwert in den Stamm —
so lass mich dich heissen
wie ich dich liebe:
Siegmund —
so nenn' ich dich.

Siegmund
(Springt auf den Stamm zu, und fasst den Schwertgriff).
Siegmund heiss' ich,
und Siegmund bin ich:
bezeug' es dies Schwert,
das zaglos ich halte!
Wälse verhiess mir,
in höchster Noth
sollt' ich es finden:
ich fass' es nun!
Heiligster Minne
höchste Noth,
sehnender Liebe
sehrende Noth,
brennt mir hell in der Brust,
drängt zu That und Tod:
Nothung! Nothung!
so nenn' ich dich Schwert —
Nothung! Nothung!
neidlicher Stahl!
Zeig' deiner Schärfe
schneidenden Zahn:
heraus aus der Scheide zu mir!
Er zieht mit einem gewaltigen Zuck das Schwert aus dem Stamme, und zeigt es der von Staunen und Entzücken erfassten *Sieglinde*.
Siegmund den Wälsung
siehst du, Weib!
Als Brautgabe
bringt er dies Schwert:
so freit er sich
die seligste Frau;
dem Feindeshaus
entführt er dich so.
Fern von hier
folge ihm nun,

forth in the smiling
softness of Spring:
there shields thee Needful, my sword,
and Siegmund but lives in thy love.
(He embraces her to draw her away with him.)

Sieglinda
(in wild intoxication).

Art thou Siegmund
standing beside me? —
Sieglinda am I,
for thee I've sighed.
Thou'st won thy sister,
I tell thee, as well as the sword.

Siegmund.

Bride and sister
be to thy brother —
so blest may the Volsungs abound!

He draws her towards him with a frenzy of passion; she sinks on his breast with a cry.—The Curtain falls quickly.

SECOND ACT.

A wild and rocky pass.

At the back a gorge slopes downwards from a high peak, the ground sinking again gradually from this towards the foreground. *Wotan* in warlike array, bearing his spear; before him stands *Brynhildr* as a "*Valkyrie*", also fully armed.

Wotan

Make ready thy steed,
stalwartest maid!
Battle's brawl
breaketh out soon:
Brynhildr, spur to the fray,
the Volsung favour and aid!
Hunding vainly sues,
void are his hopes,
in Valhall he has no place.
So headlong in haste
hie to the field.

Brynhildr
(springing from rock to rock up the height R. and shouting).

Hoyotoho! Hoyotoho!
Heiaha! Heiaha!
Hahei! Hahei! Heiaho!

(She pauses on a high peak, looks down into the gorge at back and calls to *Wotan*.)

But listen, father!
look to thyself!
thou wilt soon
suffer a storm:
watchful Fricka, thy wife
arrives in her ram-driven car.

fort in des Lenzes
lachendes Haus:
dort schützt dich Nothung das Schwert,
wenn Siegmund dir liebend erlag!
(Er umfasst sie, um sie mit sich fortzuziehen.)

Sieglinde
(in höchster Trunkenheit).

Bist du Siegmund,
den ich hier sehe —
Sieglinde bin ich,
die dich ersehnt:
die eig'ne Schwester
gewann'st du zueins mit dem Schwert!

Siegmund.

Braut und Schwester
bist du dem Bruder —
so blühe denn Wälsungen-Blut!

Er zieht sie mit wüthender Gluth an sich; sie sinkt mit einem Schrei an seine Brust. — Der Vorhang fällt schnell.

ZWEITER AUFZUG.

Wildes Felsengebirg.

Im Hintergrunde zieht sich von unten her eine Schlucht herauf, die auf ein erhöhtes Felsjoch mündet; von diesem senkt sich der Boden dem Vordergrunde zu wieder abwärts. *Wotan*, kriegerisch gewaffnet, und mit dem Speer: vor ihm *Brünnhilde*, als *Walküre*, ebenfalls in voller Waffenrüstung.

Wotan.

Nun zäume dein Ross,
reisige Maid!
Bald entbrennt
brünstiger Streit:
Brünnhilde stürme zum Kampf,
dem Wälsung kiese sie Sieg!
Hunding wähle sich,
wem er gehört:
nach Walhall taugt er mir nicht.
Drum rüstig und rasch
reite zur Wal!

Brünnhilde
(jauchzend von Fels zu Fels die Höhe rechts hinaufspringend).

Hojotoho! Hojotoho!
Heiaha! Heiaha!
Hahei! Hahei! Heiaho!

Auf einer hohen Felsspitze hält sie an, blickt in die hintere Schlucht hinab, und ruft zu *Wotan* zurück.

Dir rath' ich, Vater,
rüste dich selbst;
harten Sturm
sollst du besteh'n:
Fricka naht, deine Frau,
im Wagen mit dem Widdergespann.

Ha! how she grasps
her golden scourge!
the foolish beasts
are fainting with fear;
wheels rattling and rolling
whirl her here to the war.
In such disputes
no part I would take,
though I am happy
when heroes fight:
take heed that thou find not defeat,
for lightly I leave thee to fate!—
Hoyotoho! Hoyotoho!
Heiaha! Heiaha!
Hahei! Hahei! Hoyohei!

She has disappeared behind the montain height at side, whilst Fricka comes up from the ravine in a car drawn by two rams, and on reaching the ridge dismounts and strides hastily towards Wotan in the foreground.

Wotan
(perceiving her approach.)

The old complaints!
the old annoys!
No peace! needs I must meet them.

Fricka.
Where thou wand'rest in these wilds
thy very wife to avoid,
even here
I seek thee out,
that right to me thou may'st render.

Wotan.
Thy harass, Fricka
Fain would I hear.

Fricka.
Well I know Hunding's need;
his voice for vengeance is raised:
the queen of wedlock
hath weighed his 'quest
and wends straight
to stir thee to scourge
those rash recreants twain,
who wreaked a husband this wrong.

Wotan.
What hath wrought
of wrong this pair,
allured by Spring into love?
Their passion's fury
had frenzied them:
who mastereth Love by law?

Fricka.
How foolish and fond are thy words!
as knewest thou not, forsooth,

Hei! wie die gold'ne
Geissel sie schwingt;
die armen Thiere
ächzen vor Angst;
wild rasseln die Räder:
zornig fährt sie zum Zank!
In solchem Strausse
streit' ich nicht gern,
lieb' ich auch muthiger
Männer Schlacht:
drum sieh', wie den Sturm du bestehst;
ich Lustige lass' dich im Stich! —
Hojotoho! hojotoho!
Heiaha! heiaha!
hahei! hahei! hojohei!

Sie ist hinter der Gebirgshöhe zur Seite verschwunden, während aus der Schlucht herauf Fricka, in einem mit zwei Widdern bespannten Wagen, auf dem Joch anlangt: dort steigt sie schnell ab, und schreitet dann heftig in den Vordergrund auf Wotan zu.

Wotan
(indem er sie kommen sieht).

Der alte Sturm!
die alte Müh'!
Doch Stand muss ich ihr halten.

Fricka.
Wo in Bergen du dich birgst
der Gattin Blick zu entgeh'n,
einsam hier
such' ich dich auf,
dass Hilfe du mir verhiessest.

Wotan.
Was Fricka kümmert,
künde sie frei.

Fricka.
Ich vernahm Hunding's Noth,
um Rache rief er mich an:
der Ehe Hüterin
hörte ihn,
verhiess streng
zu strafen die That
des frech frevelnden Paar's,
das kühn den Gatten gekränkt. —

Wotan.
Was so schlimmes
schuf das Paar;
das liebend cinte der Lenz?
Der Minne Zauber
entzückte sie:
wer büsst mir der Minne Macht!

Fricka.
Wie thörig und taub du dich stellst,
als wüsstest fürwahr du nicht,

that for the blessed
conjugal bond,
discarded thus, I'm complaining!

Wotan.

Unholy
are to me oaths
which oust Love from his own;
and prithee
expect not from me
that my might should hold
where thine own is helpless;
for when strong spirits are rampant
I rouse them ever to strife.

Fricka.

Deemest thou righteous
adult'rous love?
Extend then thy license
and treat as holy
the troth plighted between
a twin-born licentious pair.
My heart and my sense
with horror consume: —
bridal embrace
of sister and brother!
When was it allowed
that love should exist 'twixt relations?

Wotan.

Now: — know it at last:
accept the shame
which hath shaped itself,
though ne'er seen was the like till to-day.
That these are true lovers
learn well from me;
to milder views then revert!
If aught of bliss
follows e'er on thy blessing
then smile in lenient love
on Siegmund and Sieglinda's troth.

Fricka.
(bursting out into violent wrath).

Dawned on us the end
of the Æsir eternal
when thou these vagrant
Volsungs begattest?
I speak straightly —
touched is thy soul?
Esteem'st thou no more
thy mightiest subjects
disdained are all things
that once were exalted,
unloosened the ties
thine own wisdom established;

dass um der Ehe
heiligen Eid,
den hart gekränkten, ich klage!

Wotan.

Unheilig
acht' ich den Eid,
der Unliebende eint;
und mir wahrlich
muthe nicht zu,
dass mit Zwang ich halte
was dir nicht haftet;
denn wo kühn Kräfte sich regen,
da rath' ich offen zum Krieg.

Fricka.

Achtest du rühmlich
der Ehe Bruch,
so prahle nun weiter
und preis' es heilig,
dass Blutschande entblüht
dem Bund eines Zwillingpaar's.
Mir schaudert das Herz,
es schwindelt mein Hirn:
bräutlich umfing
die Schwester der Bruder,
Wann — ward es erlebt'
das leiblich Geschwister sich liebten?

Wotan.

Heut' — hast du's erlebt:
erfahre so
was von selbst sich fügt,
sei zuvor auch nie es gescheh'n.
Dass jene sich lieben,
leuchtet dir hell:
drum höre redlichen Rath!
Soll süsse Lust
deinen Segen dir lohnen,
so seg'ne, lachend der Liebe,
Siegmund's und Sieglinde's Bund!

Fricka
(in höchste Entrüstung ausbrechend).

So ist es denn aus
mit den ewigen Göttern,
seit du die wilden
Wälsungen zeugtest?
Heraus sagt' ich's —
traf ich den Sinn?
Nichts gilt dir der Hehren
heilige Sippe;
hin wirfst du Alles,
was einst du geachtet;
zerreissest die Bande,
die selbst du gebunden;

lightly leav'st thou
thy hold of Heaven,
that unheld and haughty may flourish
this froward and sinful pair,
thine unfaithfulness' sensual fruit! —
O why mourn thus
o'er virtue and vows
thou hast vilely slighted thyself?
Thine own true wife
full oft hast thou wronged;
never a depth
and never a height
where thy heart longed not
lustful to rove;
while of change there lacked not to charm thee,
thou gav'st no heed to my grief.
Sorrow I bore
when thou didst forsake me,
leading to battle
the barbarous maidens
of shameless mother
born to thy blood;
for avoided so was thy wife
that this Valkyrie set,
with Brynhildr herself,
who thy voice obeys
at my potent disposal were placed.
But now that another
name takes thy fancy,
thou wand'rest wolf-like
through woodlands as "Volsung", —
now basely deigning
to such degradation
a pair of pitiful
mortals to get thee,
with these whelps of a wolf
thou wishest to humble thy wife. —
O finish thy work!
fill up the cup!
let them trample me in their triumph!

Wotan
(quietly).

Thou tak'st me not
when I would teach thee,
nor may'st thou conceive a case
demanded never till now.
Statutes only
canst thou understand;
but my full thoughts must heed
the things hitherto strange.
One thing mark thou! —
We need a man
who finds not heaven's protection,
who flieth from heavenly ties;

lösest lachend
des Himmels Haft —
dass nach Lust und Laune nur walte
dies frevelnde Zwillingspaar,
deiner Untreue zuchtlose Frucht! —
O, was klag' ich
um Ehe und Eid,
da zuerst du selbst sie versehrt!
Die treue Gattin
trogest du stets:
wo eine Tiefe,
wo eine Höhe,
dahin lugte
lüstern dein Blick,
wie des Wechsels Lust du gewänn'st,
und höhnend kränktest mein Herz!
Trauernden Sinnes
musst' ich's ertragen,
zog'st du zur Schlacht
mit den schlimmen Mädchen,
die wilder Minne
Bund dir gebar;
denn dein Weib noch scheutest du so,
dass der Walküren Schaar,
und Brünnhilde selbst,
deines Wunsches Braut,
in Gehorsam der Herrin du gab'st.
Doch jetzt, da dir neue
Namen gefielen,
als „Wälse" wölfisch
im Walde du schweiftest;
jetzt, da zu niedrigster
Schmach du dich neigtest,
gemeiner Menschen
ein Paar zu erzeugen:
jetzt dem Wurfe der Wölfin
wirfst du zu Füssen dein Weib! —
So führ' es denn aus,
fülle das Mass:
die Betrog'ne lass auch zertreten!

Wotan
(ruhig).

Nichts lerntest du,
wollt' ich dich lehren.
was nie du erkennen kannst,
eh' nicht ertagte die That.
Stets Gewohntes
nur magst du versteh'n:
doch was noch nie sich traf,
danach trachtet mein Sinn! —
Eines höre!
Noth thut ein Held,
der, ledig göttlichen Schutzes,
sich löse vom Göttergesetz:

then a charge he
alone may achieve,
which, though fain to the godhead,
the gods to effect are refused.

Fricka.

With lying spirit
wouldst thou delude me!
What help divine
could heroes e'er shape us
which to their gods were gainsaid,
by whose grace alone they may speed?

Wotan.

And their courage fearless
count'st thou for nought?

Fricka.

Who breathes this courage in them?
Who brightens the face of the faint?
Beneath thy shield
strong do they seem,
by thee bestirred
they strive in the fight;
thou — prickest these mortals,
whom thus to me thou applaud'st.
Again with falsehood
wouldst thou befool me,
with new contrivance
seeking to trick me;
but for this Volsung
in vain dost thou plead:
through him I strike at thee,
for through thee only he dares.

Wotan.

In sorrow drooping
deserted he lived:
my shield sheltered him ne'er.

Fricka.

Then shelter now withhold.
Have back the sword
upon him bestowed.

Wotan.

The sword?

Fricka.

Yes, the sword, —
the marvellous
magical sword
which the god his son hath given.

Wotan.

Siegmund has won it
himself in his need.

so nur taugt er
zu wirken die That,
die, wie noth sie den Göttern,
dem Gott doch zu wirken verwehrt.

Fricka.

Mit tiefem Sinne
willst du mich täuschen!
Was Hehres sollten
Helden je wirken,
das ihren Göttern verwehrt,
deren Gunst in ihnen nur wirkt?

Wotan.

Ihres eignen Muthes
achtest du nicht.

Fricka.

Wer hauchte Menschen ihn ein?
Wer hellte den Blöden den Blick?
In deinem Schutz
scheinen sie stark,
durch deinen Stachel
streben sie auf:
du — reizest sie einzig
die so mir Ew'gen du rühmst.
Mit neuer List
willst du mich belügen,
durch neue Ränke
jetzt mir entrinnen;
doch diesen Wälsung
gewinnst du dir nicht:
in ihm treff' ich nur dich,
denn durch dich trotzt er allein.

Wotan.

In wilden Leiden
erwuchs er sich selbst:
mein Schutz schirmte ihn nie.

Fricka.

So schütz' auch heut' ihn nicht;
nimm ihm das Schwert,
das du ihm geschenkt!

Wotan.

Das Schwert?

Fricka.

Ja — das Schwert,
das zauberstark
zuckende Schwert,
das du Gott dem Sohne gab'st.

Wotan.

Siegmund gewann es sich
selbst in der Noth.

Fricka.
Thou shapedst him the need
and the notable sword.
Dar'st thou deny it,
when night and day
I have followed thy feet?
For him struckest thou
that sword in the stem;
thou didst guard for him
the glorious blade:
be this gainsaid not,
that but by thy subtle
schemings he found the prize.
(*Wotan* makes a gesture of wrath.)
With bondsmen
no sov'reign does battle,
the monarch scourges his minion:
against thine my strength
properly strives,
but Siegmund I punish as slave.
(*Wotan* turns gloomily away.)
This slave thou holdest
wholly and closely,
to his caprice
must thy consort submit?
Shall he this shame
and infamy shape me,
to varlets a scoff —
to villians a scorn?
Sure ne'er my husband could suffer
so heinous a slight to his queen?

Wotan
(gloomily).
What requir'st thou?

Fricka.
Cast off the Volsung.

Wotan
(with choked voice.)
I give him his vent.

Fricka.
But thou — favour him not,
when to fight calls th'avenger's voice.

Wotan.
I'll — favour him not.

Fricka.
Look on me fairly,
lie not to me!
The Valkyrie vow to recal!

Wotan.
The war-maiden works untaught.

Fricka.
Du schuf'st ihm die Noth,
wie das neidliche Schwert:
willst du mich täuschen,
die Tag und Nacht
auf den Fersen dir folgt?
Für ihn stiessest du
das Schwert in den Stamm;
du verhiessest ihm
die hehre Wehr:
willst du es leugnen,
dass nur deine List
ihn lockte wo er es fänd'?
(*Wotan* macht eine Geberde des Grimmes).
Mit Unfreien
streitet kein Edler,
den Frevler straft nur der Freie:
wider deine Kraft
führt' ich wohl Krieg;
doch Siegmund verfiel mir als Knecht.
(*Wotan* wendet sich unmuthig ab.)
Der dir als Herren
hörig und eigen,
gehorchen soll ihm
dein ew'ges Gemahl?
Soll mich in Schmach
der Niedrigste schmäh'n,
den Frechen zum Sporn,
dem Freien zum Spott?
Das kann mein Gatte nicht wollen,
die Göttin entweiht es nicht so!

Wotan
(finster).
Was verlangst du?

Fricka.
Lass' von dem Wälsung!

Wotan
(mit gedämpfter Stimme).
Er geh' seines Weg's.

Fricka.
Doch du — schütze ihn nicht,
wenn zur Schlacht der Rächer ihn ruft.

Wotan.
Ich — schütze ihn nicht.

Fricka.
Sieh mir in's Auge,
sinne nicht Trug!
Die Walküre wend' auch von ihm!

Wotan.
Die Walküre walte frei.

Fricka.
Not so! 'tis thy will
she accomplishes now:
recall her from Siegmund's side!

Wotan
(after a violent inward struggle).
I cannot defeat him;
he found my sword!

Fricka.
Remove then its magic,
or bid it to break:
shieldless send him to fight.

She hears on the heights above the *Valkyrie's* call shouted by *Brynhildr*, who then appears on the rocky path R. with her horse.

Here wendeth thy warlike maid:
comes her call to my ears.

Wotan
(aside, sadly).
I made her for Siegmund to mount.

Fricka.
Thy eternal spouse's
high reputation
to-day she holdeth dear!
If laughed at in scorn,
unscreened and forlorn,
gone were the glory of gods.
Let to-day my dues
with daring and wit
be won by the mettlesome maid. —
This Volsung fell to my honour,
confirm as my victim by oath.

Wotan
(throwing himself upon a rocky seat in utter dejection and inward rage).
Take my oath!

Brynhildr, on perceiving *Fricka* from the height, suddenly breaks off her song and leads her horse by the bridle quietly and slowly down the mountain path; she has just hidden it in a cave as *Fricka* passes by her on her way to her car.

Fricka
(to *Brynhilde*).
Wotan doth
wait for thee:
let him inform thee
how the lot is to fall!

(She mounts the car and drives quickly off.)

Brynhildr
(advances with anxious and wondering looks towards *Wotan*, who, leaning back in his rocky seat, his head resting on his hand, is absorbed in gloomy reflection).
Sure, luckless
seems the strife:
Fricka laughs at the fiat! —

Fricka.
Nicht doch! deinen Willen
vollbringt sie allein:
verbiete ihr Siegmund's Sieg!

Wotan
(mit heftigem innerem Kampfe).
Ich kann ihn nicht fällen:
er fand mein Scwert!

Fricka.
Entzieh' dem den Zauber,
zerknick' es dem Knecht:
schutzlos schau' ihn der Feind!

Sie vernimmt von der Höhe her den jauchzenden Walkürenruf *Brünnhilde's:* diese erscheint dann selbst mit ihrem Ross auf dem Felspfade rechts.

Dort kommt deine kühne Maid:
jauchzend jagt sie daher.

Wotan
(dumpf für sich).
Ich rief sie für Siegmund zu Ross!

Fricka.
Deiner ew'gen Gattin
heilige Ehre
schirme heut' ihr Schild!
Von Menschen verlacht,
verlustig der Macht,
gingen wir Götter zu Grund,
würde heut' nicht hehr
und herrlich mein Recht
gerächt von der muthigen Maid. —
Der Wälsung fällt meiner Ehre: —
empfah' ich von Wotan den Eid?

Wotan
(in furchtbarem Unmuth und innerem Grimm auf einen Felsensitz sich werfend).
Nimm den Eid!

Als *Brünnhilde* von der Höhe aus *Fricka* gewahrte, brach sie schnell ihren Gesang ab, und hat nun still und langsam ihr Ross am Zügel den Felsweg herabgeleitet; sie birgt dieses jetzt in einer Höhle, als *Fricka*, zu ihrem Wagen sich zurückwendend, an ihr vorbeischreitet.

Fricka
(zu *Brünnhilde*).
Heervater
harret dein :
lass' ihn dir künden
wie er das Loos gekies't!

(Sie besteigt den Wagen, und fährt schnell nach hinten davon.)

Brünnhilde.
(tritt mit verwunderter und besorgter Miene vor *Wotan*. der, auf dem Felssitz zurückgelehnt, das Haupt auf die Hand gestützt, in finstres Brüten versunken ist).
Schlimm, fürcht' ich,
schloss der Streit,
lachte Fricka dem Loose! —

Father, what must
thy child fulfil thee?
Sad and downcast thou seemest.

Wotan
(letting his arms fall powerless and his head sink on his breast).

My own the fetters
fast'ning me: —
I, less free than the earth-born!

Brynhildr.
I saw thee thus ne'er!
What gnaws at thy heart?

Wotan
(flinging up his arms in wild despair).

O greatest of shame!
O shunless disgrace!
Gods' distress!
Gods' distress!
Endless regret!
Infinite grief!
The saddest am I among all men!

Brynhildr
(terrified, throws away her shield, spear and helmet and sinks at *Wotan's* feet in anxious affection).

Father! Father!
Tell me what ails thee!
See how trembles with terror thy child!
O trust in me,
thy daughter true!
Lo! Brynhildr beggeth!
(She lays her head and hands confidingly and anxiously on his knees and breast.)

Wotan
(gazes into her eyes for a long while, and strokes her hair; then, as if awaking from a deep reverie, he begins at last in a very faint voice).

If it were uttered
I should lay bare
ev'ry secret hold of my heart.

Brynhildr
(replying in the same low voice).

To Wotan's will thou speakest;
tell me then what thou wilt.
What am I
when I'm away from thee?

Wotan.
What lies in my breast unrelated,
eke must remain
unspoken for ever:
myself I talk with,
telling to thee — — —

Vater, was soll
dein Kind erfahren?
Trübe scheinst du und traurig!

Wotan
(lässt den Arm machtlos sinken und den Kopf in den Nacken fallen.)

In eig'ner Fessel
fing ich mich: —
ich unfreiester Aller!

Brünnhilde.
So sah ich dich nie!
Was nagt dir das Herz?

Wotan
(in wildem Ausbruche den Arm erhebend).

O heilige Schmach!
O schmählicher Harm!
Götternoth!
Götternoth!
Endloser Grimm!
Ewiger Gram!
Der Traurigste bin ich von Allen!

Brünnhilde
(wirft erschrocken Schild, Speer und Helm von sich, und lässt sich mit besorgter Zutraulichkeit zu *Wotan's* Füssen nieder).

Vater! Vater!
Sage, was ist dir?
Wie erschreck'st du mit Sorge dein Kind!
Vertraue mir:
ich bin dir treu;
sieh', Brünnhilde bittet!
(Sie legt traulich und ängstlich Haupt und Hände ihm auf Knie und Schoss).

Wotan
blickt ihr lange in's Auge, und streichelt ihr dann die Locken: wie aus tiefem Sinnen zu sich kommend, beginnt er endlich mit sehr leiser Stimme).

Lass' ich's verlauten,
lös' ich dann nicht
meines Willens haltenden Haft?

Brünnhilde
(ihm eben so leise erwidernd).

Zu Wotan's Willen sprichst du,
sagst du mir was du willst:
wer — bin ich,
wär' ich dein Wille nicht?

Wotan.
Was Keinem in Worten ich künde,
unausgesprochen
bleib' es ewig:
mit mir nur rath' ich,
red' ich zu dir. — — —

(With voice still more suppressed and awful, while he still gazes fixedly into *Brynhildr's* eyes.)
When youthful love's
  illusions had fled
then lusted my soul for sway:
impelled by wildest
  wishes for power
I won to me the world.
  Scarce witting ill,
  I stooped to deception,
  covenants ordered
  that stretched to crime.
Loki allured me with lying,
then faithlessly he fled. —
  And yet Love I would
  fain not relinquish;
through all fame I longed for affection.
  In night's abode
  the baleful Nibelung,
Alberic, broke from its bonds.
  He cursed at Love's passion,
  and won by the curse
the Rhine-nymphs' glittering gold,
and mastered measureless might.
  The ring which he shaped
  I ravished by cunning;
  but ne'er I rendered it
  back to the Rhine:
  it was the handsel
  of Valhalla,
the burg that giants had built me,
from which now all kingdoms I bend.
  That able witch,
  who all things wist,
  Erda, most wise
  and wondrous of women,
reded ill of the ring,
warned me of awfullest ending.
  Then this ending I longed
  more to learn of,
but silent the seer took leave.
So departed my peace of mind,
and wisdom I strove to possess:
  to the depths of earth
  diving in my search,
  by love I won
  the witch to my purpose,
mastered her potent might,
that to me she oped her mind.
  Sooth-sayings plainly she spoke,
  in payment bearing my pledge:
  the world's wonder of women
  bore thee, Brynhildr, to me.
    With eight sisters
    wert thou brought up;
    in these Valkyries'
    valiant virtue

(Mit noch gedämpfterer, schauerlicher Stimme, während er *Brünnhilden* unverwandt in das Auge blickt.)
Als junger Liebe
  Lust mir verblich,
verlangte nach Macht mein Muth:
  von jäher Wünsche
  Wüthen gejagt,
gewann ich mir die Welt,
  Unwissend trugvoll
  übt' ich Untreue,
  band durch Verträge,
  was Unheil barg:
listig verlockte mich Loge,
der schweifend nun verschwand. —
  Von der Liebe doch
  mocht' ich nicht lassen;
in der Macht gehrt' ich nach Minne:
  den Nacht gebar,
  der bange Nibelung,
Alberich brach ihren Bund;
  er fluchte der Liebe,
  und gewann durch den Fluch
des Rheines glänzendes Gold
und mit ihm masslose Macht.
  Den Reif, den er schuf,
  entriss ich ihm listig:
  doch nicht dem Rhein
  gab ich ihn zurück;
  mit ihm bezahlt' ich
  Walhall's Zinnen,
der Burg, die Riesen mir bauten,
aus der ich der Welt nun gebot. —
  Die Alles weiss,
  was einstens war,
  Erda, die weihlich
  weiseste Wala,
rieth mir ab von dem Ring,
warnte vor ewigem Ende.
  Von dem Ende wollt' ich
  mehr noch wissen;
doch schweigend entschwand mir das Weib.
Da verlor ich den leichten Muth;
zu wissen begehrt es den Gott;
  in den Schoos der Welt
  schwang ich mich hinab,
  mit Liebes-Zauber
  zwang ich die Wala,
  stört' ihres Wissens Stolz,
dass sie nun Rede mir stand.
  Kunde empfing ich von ihr:
  von mir doch barg sie ein Pfand:
  der Welt weisestes Weib
  gebar mir, Brünnhilde, dich.
    Mit acht Schwestern
    zog ich dich auf:
    durch euch Walküren
    wollt' ich wenden,

viewed I a vent
from impending doom: —
a dolorous end to the Æsir.
That foes might find us
strong for the strife,
heroes I bade ye select me:
the bravest of hearts
we had held in bondage,
those mortals whom
in their might we had checked,
who by guileful agreements'
glamour and baseness
obedient served us
truly and blindly, —
these should ye bestir
to stormiest striving,
ev'ry force guiding
to grimmest fight,
that flocks of fearless heroes
might hail me in Valhall's hall.

Brynhildr.
And thy hall mightily filled we:
many a man have I brought.
Whence comes thy depression?
We never have paused.

Wotan.
Another ache: —
earnestly weigh
what more the witch hath forewarned!
Through Alberic's host
threatens our ending;
still nourishing wrath
rages the Nibelung;
I shrink not though now
from his nation of shadows,
by my heroes shielded and safe.
But if e'er the wretch
the ring should recover,
our high Valhalla were lost then.
He who love surrendered,
he alone
evil ends·
by the ring can wreak,
and to all of us
unending disgrace.
My heroes' might
were ravished from me,
my friends themselves
were turned into foes,
whom he would force
to fight against me.
So I set to myself
to keep the ring from his clutches:

was mir die Wala
zu fürchten schuf —
ein schmähliches Ende der Ew'gen.
Dass stark zum Streit
uns fände der Feind,
hiess ich euch Helden mir schaffen:
die herrisch wir sonst
in Gesetzen hielten,
die Männer, denen
den Muth wir gewehrt,
die durch trüber Verträge
trügende Bande
zu blindem Gehorsam,
wir uns gebunden —
die solltet zu Sturm
und Streit ihr nun stacheln,
ihre Kraft reizen
zu rauhem Krieg,
dass kühner Kämpfer Schaaren
ich sammle in Walhall's Saal.

Brünnhilde.
Deinen Saal füllten wir weidlich;
viele schon führt' ich dir zu.
Was macht dir nun Sorge,
da nie wir gesäumt?

Wotan.
Ein Andres ist's:
achte es wohl,
wess' mich die Wala gewarnt! —
Durch Alberich's Heer
droht uns das Ende:
in neidischem Grimm
grollt mir der Niblung;
doch scheu' ich nun nicht
seine nächtlichen Schaaren —
meine Helden schüfen mir Sieg.
Nur wenn je den Ring
zurück er gewänne —
dann wäre Walhall verloren.
der der Liebe fluchte,
ihn allein
nützte neidisch
des Ringes Runen
zu aller Edlen
endloser Schmach;
der Helden Muth
.entwendet' er mir;
die Kühnen selber
zwäng' er zum Kampf,
mit ihrer Kraft
bekriegte er mich.
Sorgend sann ich nun selbst
den Ring dem Feind zu entreissen:

the craftsman huge,
to whom as his hire
my compact gave
the accurséd gold —
Fafnir holdeth the hoard,
to gain which his brother he felled.
From him must the ring be wrested,
although for wage 'twas awarded:
but my treaty with him
restrains me from harming;
moveless and weak
'gainst him is my might.
These are the chains
which thrall and chafe me:
I, who by treaty have reigned
to my treaties now become slave.
But one may compass
what I must leave:
a hero helped
by none of our number,
who finds no guide
or friend in the gods, —
unawares,
under no stress,
from out his need,
by his own design
works out the deed
which I would have done,
of which my tongue ne'er told,
though ever first in my thoughts. —
He who 'gainst ev'ry god
fights yet for me,
this friendliest foe,
how find him indeed?
How shall I affect one
whom ne'er I shielded,
who in his defiance
is faithful to me?
How master another,
who, not mine own,
from out his will
for my ends shall work? —
O godly distress!
Grievous reproach!
Abhorrent to
my heart have I found
each hazard wild I have worked for!
Another end I have sighed for,
that other I seek in vain;
unswayed must a freeman assist me —
near me are nothing but slaves.

Brynhildr.

But the Volsung, Siegmund,
works by himself?

der Riesen einer,
denen ich einst
mit verfluchtem Gold
den Fleiss vergalt,
Fafner hütet den Hort,
um den er den Bruder gefällt.
Ihm müsst' ich den Reif entringen,
den selbst als Zoll ich ihm zahlte:
doch mit dem ich vertrug,
ihn darf ich nicht treffen;
machtlos vor ihm
erläge mein Muth.
Das sind die Bande,
die mich binden:
der durch Verträge ich Herr,
den Verträgen bin ich nun Knecht.
Nur Einer dürfte
was ich nicht darf:
ein Held, dem helfend
nie ich mich neigte;
der fremd dem Gotte
frei seiner Gunst,
unbewusst,
ohne Geheiss,
aus eig'ner Noth
mit der eig'nen Wehr
schüfe die That,
die ich scheuen muss,
die nie mein Rath ihm rieth,
wünscht sie auch einzig mein Wunsch. —
Der entgegen dem Gott
für mich föchte,
den freundlichen Feind,
wie fänd' ich ihn?
Wie schüf' ich den Freien,
den nie ich schirmte,
der in eig'nem Trotze
der Trauteste mir?
Wie macht' ich den Andren,
der nicht mehr ich,
und aus sich wirkte,
was ich nur will? —
O göttliche Schmach!
O schählmiche Noth!
Zum Ekel find' ich
ewig nur mich
in Allem was ich erwirke!
Das Andre, das ich ersehne,
das Andre erseh' ich nie;
denn selbst muss der Freie sich schaffen—
Knechte erknet' ich mir nur!

Brünnhilde.

Doch der Wälsung, Siegmund?
wirkt er nicht selbst?

DIE WALKUERE.

Wotan.

Wildly roving
with him through woodlands,
'gainst ev'ry godly rede
roused I ever his hate —
'gainst ev'ry godly rancour
shields him now only the sword,
that as a grace
a god has bestowed. —
How to myself
my craft was deceptive!
So swiftly hath Fricka
found out the lie!
She looked me through
and thrust on me shame:
I perforce must shape to her fiat!

Brynhildr.

The vict'ry from Siegmund thou'llt snatch?

Wotan
(in an outburst of wild despair).

I have wrested Alberic's ring, —
grasped the coveted gold!
The curse I incurred
doth cling to me yet: —
what I love best I must relinquish,
slay him I hold most sacred,
trusting belief
foully betray! —
Glory and fame
fade from my sight!
Heavenly splendour,
smiling disgrace!
Be laid in ruins
all I have reared!
Over is my work:
but one thing waits me now —
the ending — —
the ending! —
(He pauses and reflects.)
And for that ending
looks Alberic! —
Now I measure
the meaning mute
of what the witch spake in wisdom: —
"When that Love's defiant foe
grimly getteth a son,
the sway of gods
full soon shall end!" —
The Niblung dwarf
I now understand
to have won to him a woman,
by gold gaining his hopes.

Wotan.

Wild durchschweift' ich
mit ihm die Wälder;
gegen der Götter Rath
reizte kühn ich ihn auf —
gegen der Götter Rache
schützt ihn nun einzig das Schwert,
das eines Gottes
Gunst ihm beschied —
Wie wollt' ich listig
selbst mich belügen?
So leicht entfrug mir
ja Fricka den Trug!
Zu tiefster Scham
durchschaute sie mich:
ihrem Willen muss ich gewähren!

Brünnhilde.

So nimmst du von Siegmund den Sieg?

Wotan
(in wildem Schmerz der Verzweiflung ausbrechend).

Ich berührte Alberich's Ring —
gierig hielt ich das Gold!
Der Fluch, den ich floh,
nicht flieht er nun mich: —
was ich liebe, muss ich verlassen,
morden, was je ich minne,
trügend verrathen
wer mir vertraut! —
Fahre denn hin,
herrische Pracht,
göttlichen Prunkes
prahlende Schmach!
Zusammen breche
was ich gebaut!
Auf geb' ich mein Werk,
Eines nur will ich noch,
das Ende — —
das Ende! —
(Er hält sinnend ein.)
Und für das Ende
sorgt Alberich! —
jetzt versteh' ich
den stummen Sinn
des wilden Wortes der Wala: —
„Wenn der Liebe finstrer Feind
zürnend zeugt einen Sohn,
der Seligen Ende
säumt dann nicht!"
Vom Niblung ;·
vernahm ich
dass ein Weib
dess' Guns+

In lust she bears,
loveless, a babe
and hatred's fruit
from her draws life.
The love-scorner well
can work such wonders;
but he I long for fondly —
the free one — doth lack to me yet!
(Wrathfully.)
Then now take my blessing,
Nibelung's babe!
What thus I fling from me
hold as thy fortune —
Valhalla's sumptuous halls
shall sate thy unhallowed desires!

Brynhildr
(terrified).

O speak, father!
What should I perform?

Wotan
(bitterly).

Fight duly for Fricka,
champion her virgin vows!
What she commands
is my bidding too.
How fruitless is my volition,
since a free man ne'er I may light on! —
For Fricka's vassal
victory shape!

Brynhildr.

Woe! retract,
I entreat, thy word!
Thou lov'st Siegmund;
for this love —
I wot well — should I o'erwatch him.

Wotan.

Vanquish Siegmund surely:
to Hunding the vict'ry assign!
Heed thyself well,
and hold thyself strong;
bring all thy bravery
duly to bear:
a sooth-sword
swings Siegmund —
scarcely canst thou o'ercome.

Brynhildr.

One thou hast bade me
ever to bless,
whose unwonted firmness
awakes thy affection,
from his side moves me never
thy mandate constrained.

Des Hasses Frucht
hegt eine Frau;
des Neides Kraft
kreiss't ihr im Schosse:
das Wunder gelang
dem Liebelosen;
doch der in Liebe ich frei'te,
den Freien erlang' ich mir nie! —
(Grimmig.)
So nimm meinen Segen,
Niblungen-Sohn!
Was tief mich ekelt,
dir geb' ich's zum Erbe,
der Gottheit nichtigen Glanz:
zernage sie gierig dein Neid!

Brünnhilde
(erschrocken).

O sag', künde!
Was soll nun dein Kind?

Wotan
(bitter.)

Fromm streite für Fricka,
hüte ihr Ehe und Eide!
Was sie erkor,
das kiese auch ich.
Was frommte mir eig'ner Wille?
Einen Freien kann ich nicht wollen —
für Fricka's Knechte
kämpfe du nun!

Brünnhilde.

Weh! nimm reuig
zurück das Wort!
Du liebst Siegmund:
dir zu Lieb' —
ich weiss es — schütz' ich den Wälsung.

Wotan.

Fällen sollst du Siegmund,
für Hunding erfechten den Sieg!
Hüte dich wohl
und halte dich stark;
all deiner Kühnheit
entbiete im Kampf:
ein Sieg-Schwert
schwingt Siegmund —
schwerlich fällt er dir feig.

Brünnhilde.

Den du zu lieben
stets mich gelehrt,
der in hehrer Tugend
dem Herzen dir theuer —
gegen ihn zwingt mich nimmer
dein zwiespältig Wort.

Wotan.
Ha, froward child!
floutest thou me?
What art thou else but the willing
blind wand of my pow'r?
Now my woe thou hast learnt,
have I sunk so low
that my very servant
should venture to scorn?
Child, would'st challenge my wrath?
Thy courage were vain,
if ever vented
on thee sternly it struck!
Within my bosom
burneth a rage
which could, reckless, work
woe to a world
that once I looked on in love: —
tremble, all, at its flash!
Fearful vengeance shall fall! —
I warn thee then
wake not mine ire:
my sentence heed and fulfil. —
Siegmund falleth!
Brynhild' must work out my will.
(He rushes off and disappears L. in the mountains.)

Brynhildr
(stands for some time shocked and stupified).
So — spake
my sire ne'er before,
though stirred and shaken by strife!
(Troubled, she stoops and picks up her weapons with which she arms herself again.)
How waxes
my weapons' weight! —
When I love the fight
how lightly they lift! —
I fear to seek
such and evil fray! —
(She reflects and then heaves a sigh.)
Ha, my hero!
In grievous strait
thy defender must falsely forsake thee! —
She turns up the stage and perceives *Siegmund* and *Sieglinda* as they mount from the valley: she watches their approach a moment and then goes into the cavern to her horse, so that she completely disappears from sight of the audience.

Siegmund and *Sieglinda* enter. She presses hastily forwards; he seeks to restrain her.

Siegmund.
Pause here awhile:
take some repose!

Sieglinda.
Farther! Farther!

Wotan.
Ha, Freche du!
frevelst du mir?
Was bist du, als meines Willens
blind wählende Kür? —
Da mit dir ich tagte,
sank ich so tief,
dass zum Schimpf der eig'nen
Geschöpfe ich ward?
Kennst du Kind meinen Zorn?
Verzage dein Muth,
wenn je zermalmend
auf dich stürzte sein Strahl!
In meinem Busen
berg' ich den Grimm,
der in Grauen und Wust
wirft eine Welt,
die einst zur Lust mir gelacht: —
wehe dem, den er trifft!
Trauer schüf' ihm sein Trotz! —
Drum rath' ich dir,
reize mich nicht:
besorge was ich befahl:
Siegmund falle! —
Dies sei der Walküre Werk.
(Er stürmt fort, und verschwindet schnell links im Gebirge.)

Brünnhilde
(steht lange betäubt und erschrocken).
So — sah ich
Siegvater nie,
erzürnt' ihn sonst auch ein Zank!
(Sie neigt sich betrübt und nimmt ihre Waffen auf, mit denen sie sich wieder rüstet.)
Schwer wiegt mir
der Waffen Wucht: —
wenn nach Lust ich focht,
wie waren sie leicht! —
Zu böser Schlacht
schleich' ich heut' so bang! —
(Sie sinnt, und seufzt dann auf.)
Weh', mein Wälsung!
Im höchsten Leid
muss dich treulos die Treue verlassen! —
Sie wendet sich nach hinten, und gewahrt *Siegmund* und *Sieglinde*, wie sie aus der Schlucht heraufsteigen: sie betrachtet die Nahenden einen Augenblick, und wendet sich dann in die Höhle zu ihrem Ross, so dass sie dem Zuschauer gänzlich verschwindet.

Siegmund und *Sieglinde* treten auf. Sie schreitet hastig voraus; er sucht sie aufzuhalten.

Siegmund.
Raste nun hier:
gönne dir Ruh'!

Sieglinde.
Weiter! Weiter!

Siegmund
(clasping her with tender restraint).
No farther now!
O linger, sweet one, at last! —
From loving embraces
brok'st thou away,
with sudden haste.
sallying forth;
scarce found I thy way of flight:
through wood and field,
over fell and steep,
speechless — silent
speeding along:
my voice lured thee in vain.
(She stares wildly before her.)
Onward no more;
open thy lips!
End me this silent awe!
See, thy brother
holdeth his bride: —
Siegmund's guarding thee safe.
(He has led her, without her noticing it, to the rocky seat.)

Sieglinda
(gazes into *Siegmund's* eyes with growing rapture, then mournfully hangs upon his neck. At last she starts up with a sudden panic, while *Siegmund* hastily clasps her).
Away! Away!
flee from the wanton!
Unholily
fold thee mine arms;
disgraced — polluted,
life ebbeth forth.
Shun the foul one,
fly from her face!
Her dust tempests shall drive,
who, soiled, gave herself to thine arms! —

When in thy loving embrace
with hallowed delight I brimm'd,
my only husband was he
who all my heart had awaked. —
From this heavenly rapture's
glorious radiance,
which all my soul
and senses o'erwhelmed,
shudder and trembling
and shamefullest terrors
grimly o'ertook
the traitorous woman,
who to a bridegroom belonged,
whom she obeyed without love.
Leave the accurst one,
let her escape!
I rest degraded,
bereft of grace!
The pearl of manhood
must I depart from;

Siegmund
(umfasst sie mit sanfter Gewalt).
Nicht weiter nun!
Verweile, süssestes Weib! —
Aus Wonne-Entzücken
zucktest du auf,
mit jäher Hast
jagtest du fort;
kaum folgt' ich der wilden Flucht:
durch Wald und Flur,
über Fels und Stein,
sprachlos schweigend
sprangst du dahin;
zur Rast hielt dich kein Ruf.
(Sie starrt wild vor sich hin.)
Ruhe nun aus:
rede zu mir!
Ende des Schweigens Angst!
Sieh, dein Bruder
hält seine Braut:
Siegmund ist dir Gesell!
(Er hat sie unvermerkt nach dem Steinsitze geleitet.)

Sieglinde
(blickt *Siegmund* mit wachsendem Entzücken in die Augen; dann umschlingt sie leidenschaftlich seinen Hals. Endlich fährt sie mit jähem Schreck auf, während *Siegmund* sie heftig fasst).
Hinweg! hinweg!
flieh' die Entweihte!
Unheilig
umfasst dich mein Arm;
entehrt, geschändet
schwand dieser Leib:
flieh' die Leiche,
lasse sie los!
der Wind mag sie verweh'n,
die ehrlos dem Edlen sich gab! — —

Da er sie liebend umfing,
da seligste Lust sie fand,
da ganz sie minnte der Mann,
der ganz ihr Minne geweckt —
vor der süssesten Wonne
heiligster Weihe,
die ganz ihr Sinne
und Seele durchdrang,
Grauen und Schauder
ob grässlichster Schande
musste mit Schreck
die Schmähliche fassen,
die je dem Manne gehorcht,
der ohne Minne sie hielt! —
Lass' die Verfluchte,
lass' sie dich flieh'n!
Verworfen bin ich,
der Würde bar!
Dir reinstem Manne
muss ich entrinnen;

for ne'er may I link me
with one so noble:
shame I bring to my brother, —
shape my rescuer's ruin.

Siegmund.

Who erst shaped for thee shame
shall bring me his felon blood!
So fly me no further,
halt for the foeman;
here — shall I defeat him.—
When "Needful"
at his heart shall gnaw,
then revenge thou shalt attain!

Sieglinda
(starting up and listening).

Hark! the horncalls —
Hearest thou not?
Nearer still
waxes the sound;
from wood and vale
voices arise;
Hunding hath wakened
from heavy sleep;
sleuth-hounds and hunters
bids he assemble:
roused by his hail
howls the rabble,
all crying to heaven
for the breaking of conjugal bonds!

(She laughs madly, — then suddenly shrinks in terror.)

Where art thou, Siegmund?
Still art thou near?
Bridegroom beloved,
lordiest brother!
Let thy star-like eyes
yet but stream light upon me;
wend not away
from a woeful woman's kiss! —
Hark, oh hark!
that is Hunding's horn!
And his men approach
in mighty force.
No sword that pack
of hounds can scare: —
cast it forth, Siegmund! —
Siegmund — where art thou? —
Ha! there — I see thee now —
sinister sight! —
Dogs are mouthing
and gnashing for meat;
no heed they take
of thy hero glance;

dir herrlichem darf ich
nimmer gehören:
Schande bring' ich dem Bruder,
Schmach dem freienden Freund!

Siegmund.

Was je Schande dir schuf,
das büsst nun des Frevlers Blut!
Drum fliehe nicht weiter;
harre des Feindes;
hier — soll er mir fallen:
wenn Nothung ihm
das Herz zernagt,
Rache dann hast du erreicht!

Sieglinde
(schrickt auf und lauscht).

Horch! die Hörner —
hörst du den Ruf? —
Ringsher tönt
wüthend Getös";
aus Wald und Gau
gellt es herauf.
Hunding erwachte
von hartem Schlaf;
Sippen und Hunde
ruft er zusammen:
muthig gehetzt
heult die Meute,
wild bellt sie zum Himmel
um der Ehe gebrochenen Eid!

(Sie lacht wie wahnsinnig auf: — dann schrickt sie ängstlich zusammen.)

Wo bist du, Siegmund?
seh' ich dich noch?
brünstig geliebter
leuchtender Bruder!
Deines Auges Stern
lass noch einmal mir strahlen:
wehre dem Kuss
des verworf'nen Weibes nicht!—
Horch! o horch!
das ist Hunding's Horn!
Seine Meute naht
mit mächtiger Wehr.
Kein Schwert frommt
vor der Hunde Schwall: —
wirf es fort, Siegmund!
Siegmund — wo bist du? —
Ha dort — ich sehe dich —
schrecklich Gesicht! —
Rüden fletschen
die Zähne nach Fleisch;
sie achten nicht
deines edlen Blick's;

in thy feet they bury
their furious teeth —
thou fall'st —
to splinters doth spring thy sword: —
the ashtree splits —
both branch and stem! —
Brother! my brother!
Siegmund — ha! —

(With a cry she falls senseless in *Siegmund's* arms.)

Siegmund.
Sister! Belov'd one!

He listens for her breathing and satisfies himself that she still lives. He allows her to slip down with him, so that while he sinks to a sitting position her head rests on his knees. In this position they remain till the end of the following scene.
Long silence, during which *Siegmund* bends over *Sieglinda* in tender care and impresses a long kiss on her brow. —
Brynhilda, leading her horse by the bridle advances slowly and solemnly towards the front and stands beside *Siegmund*, a little apart from him. She bears her shield and spear in one hand, rests the other on her horse's neck, and thus, in grave silence, watches *Siegmund* awhile.

Brynhildr.
Siegmund! —
See'st thou me? —
I — come
to call thee hence.

Siegmund
(raising his eyes to her).
Declare thy name,
who dost stand so beauteous and stern.

Brynhildr.
But fated men
my form may look on:
to whom 'tis shewn
full shortly must leave this life.
On the war-plain alone
the warrior sees me:
well then he weens
away must he with me.

Siegmund
(looks long into her eyes, then bows his head in thought and at last turns again towards her with solemn earnestness).
But firstly tell,
whither tak'st thou the hero?

Brynhildr.
To Wotan,
for such is his will:
hence with me!
Awaits Valhall' for thee.

Siegmund.
In Valhall's bright vault
shall I find him alone?

bei den Füssen packt dich
das feste Gebiss —
du fällst —
in Stücken zerstaucht das Schwert: —
die Esche stürzt —
es bricht der Stamm! —
Bruder! mein Bruder.
Siegmund — ha! —

(Sie sinkt mit einem Schrei ohnmächtig in *Siegmund's* Arme.)

Siegmund.
Schwester! Geliebte!

Er lauscht ihrem Athem, und überzeugt sich, dass sie noch lebe. Er lässt sie an sich herabgleiten, so dass sie, als er sich selbst zum Sitze niederlässt, mit ihrem Haupt auf seinem Schoss zu ruhen kommt. In dieser Stellung verbleiben beide bis zum Schlusse des folgenden Auftrittes.
Langes Schweigen, während dessen *Siegmund* mit zärtlicher Sorge über *Sieglinde* sich hinneigt, und mit einem langen Kusse ihr die Stirn küsst. —
Brünnhilde ist, ihr Ross am Zaume geleitend, aus der Höhle langsam und feierlich nach vorne geschritten, und hält nun, *Siegmund* zur Seite, in geringer Entfernung von ihm. Sie trägt Schild und Speer in der einen Hand, lehnt sich mit der andren an den Hals des Rosses, und betrachtet so, in ernstem Schweigen, eine Zeit lang *Siegmund.*

Brünnhilde.
Siegmund! —
Sieh' auf mich!
Ich — bin's,
der bald du folgst.

Siegmund
(richtet den Blick zu ihr auf).
Wer bist du, sag',
die so schön und ernst mir erscheint?

Brünnhilde.
Nur Todgeweihten
taugt mein Anblick:
wer mich erschaut,
der scheidet vom Lebens-Licht.
Auf der Walstatt allein
erschein' ich Edlen:
wer mich gewahrt,
zur Wal kor ich ihn mir.

Siegmund
(blickt ihr lange in das Auge, senkt dann sinnend das Haupt und wendet sich endlich mit feierlichem Ernste wieder zu ihr).
Der dir nun folgt,
wohin führst du den Helden?

Brünnhilde.
Zu Walvater,
der dich gewählt,
führ' ich dich:
nach Walhall folgst du mir.

Siegmund.
In Walhall's Saal
Walvater find' ich allein?

Brynhildr.
The fallen heroes'
hallowed band
shall flock, with hand
and heart hailing thy sight.

Siegmund.
Fareth in Valhall
Volsung, my noble father?

Brynhildr.
Thy father findest thou,
Volsung, there.

Siegmund.
Shall I in Valhall'
welcome a wife.

Brynhildr.
Wish-maidens
wait on thee there:
Wotan's daughter
faithfully deals thee the drink.

Siegmund.
High thou art
and holy: I ween
thou art Wotan's child.
Yet tell me one thing, and truly!
Attendeth her brother
my bride and my sister?
shall there Siegmund
Sieglinda find?

Brynhildr.
Lone on earth
must she still linger:
Sieglinda
will see Siegmund no more!

Siegmund.
Then greet for me Valhall',
greet for me Wotan,
greet for me Volsung
and all the heroes —
greet too the high-born
wish-maidens:
to them I'll follow thee not.

Brynhildr.
Thou'st looked on the Valkyrie's
life-quelling face;
with her thou must away.

Brünnhilde.
Gefall'ner Helden
hehre Schaar
umfängt dich hold
mit hoch-heiligem Gruss.

Siegmund.
Fänd' ich in Walhall
Wälse, den eig'nen Vater?

Brünnhilde.
Den Vater findet
der Wälsung dort.

Siegmund.
Grüsst mich in Walhall
froh eine Frau?

Brünnhilde.
Wunschmädchen
walten dort hehr:
Wotan's Tochter
reicht dir traulich den Trank.

Siegmund.
Hehr bist du:
heilig gewahr' ich
das Wotanskind:
doch Eines sag' mir, du Ew'ge!
Begleitet den Bruder
die bräutliche Schwester?
umfängt Siegmund
Sieglinde dort?

Brünnhilde.
Erdenluft
muss sie noch athmen:
Sieglinde
sieht Siegmund dort nicht!

Siegmund.
So grüsse mir Walhall,
grüsse mir Wotan,
grüsse mir Wälse
und alle Helden —
grüss' auch die holden
Wunsches-Mädchen:
zu ihnen folg' ich dir nicht.

Brünnhilde.
Du sah'st der Walküre
sehrenden Blick:
mit ihr musst du nun zieh'n!

Siegmund.
Where Sieglinda bides
in bliss or bane
there will Siegmund too sojourn:
not yet hath thy sight
weakened my spirit:
'twill stir me never away.

Brynhildr.
While life doth last
dauntless thou art;
'gainst Death 'twere foolish to fight: —
and to announce him
now I come.

Siegmund.
What hero is he
by whom I fall.

Brynhildr.
Hunding fells thee in strife.

Siegmund.
Bring stronger menace
than Hunding's struggle!
Swoopest thou here
seeking thy prey,
choose my foeman for spoil:
I purpose to slay him in fight.

Brynhildr
(shaking her head).
Thou, Volsung —
hark to my voice! —
thou art to death consigned.

Siegmund.
See'st thou this sword?
By one 'twas sent
who'll shape success.
I defy thee, firm in its strength.

Brynhildr
(loudly raising her voice).
He who bestowed it
shapes thee now death:
he withdraws the charm from the sword.

Siegmund
(quickly).
Soft! disturb not
my slumbering love! —

(He bends tenderly over *Sieglinda* with an outburst of anguish.)

Woe! Woe!
Loveliest one!
Thou saddest and faithfullest sister!

Siegmund.
Wo Sieglinde lebt
in Lust und Leid,
da will Siegmund auch säumen:
noch machte dein Blick
nicht mich erbleichen:
vom Bleiben zwingt er mich nie!

Brünnhilde.
So lange du lebst
zwäng' dich wohl nichts;
doch zwingt dich Thoren der Tod: —
ihn dir zu künden
kam ich her.

Siegmund.
Wo wäre der Held,
dem heut' ich fiel?

Brünnhilde.
Hunding fällt dich im Streit.

Siegmund.
Mit stärk'rem drohe
als Hunding's Streichen!
Lauerst du hier
lüstern auf Wal.
jenen kiese zum Fang:
ich denk' ihn zu fällen im Kampf.

Brünnhilde
(den Kopf schüttelnd).
Dir, Wälsung —
höre mich wohl! —
dir ward das Loos gekies't.

Siegmund.
Kennst du diess Schwert?
Der mir es schuf,
beschied mir Sieg:
deinem Drohen trotz' ich mit ihm!

Brünnhilde
(mit stark erhobener Stimme).
Der dir es schuf,
beschied dir jetzt Tod:
seine Tugend nimmt er dem Schwert!

Siegmund
(heftig).
Schweig', und schrecke
die Schlummernde nicht! —

(Er beugt sich, mit hervorbrechendem Schmerze, zärtlich über *Siegunde*.)

Weh! Weh!
Du süssestes Weib!
Du traurigste aller Getreuen!

'Gainst thy peace wantonly
warreth the world;
and I, on whom only thou lean'st,
for whom thou hast ev'rything left,
I may not shield
nor seek thee a shelter,
but fail thee, alas! in the fight. —
O shame on him
who bestowed the sword
to shape me such shifting shield!
If I must perish
I'll pass not to Valhall': —
Hella hold me her prey!

Brynhildr
(shocked).

Celestial splendours then
spurn'st thou so lightly?
Is this woman
thy only wealth,
who faint and ailing
feebly reclines in thine arms?
Nought else deemest thou dear?

Siegmund
(bitterly looking up at her).

So young and fair
thy features appear,
but how cold and hard
accounts thee my heart! —
Canst thou not help me,
then hie thee away,
thou harsh, unwavering maid!
If moved not to pity
by my despair
then freely feast on my woe;
let my pangs flatter
thy pitiless heart; —
but of Valhall's paltry virtues
prythee vaunt not to me!

Brynhildr
(with increasing emotion).

I see the distress
of thy heart at this strait,
I feel for the hardy
hero's illhap: — —
Siegmund, to me trust thy wife;
I'll shield her much as I may!

Siegmund.

No other than I
shall in life defend my beloved;
if fate wills it so,
I will slay her slumbering first!

Gegen dich wüthet
in Waffen die Welt:
und ich, dem du einzig vertraut,
für den du ihr einzig getrotzt —
mit meinem Schutz
nicht soll ich dich schirmen,
die Kühne verrathen im Kampf? —
O Schande ihm,
der das Schwert mir schuf,
beschied er mir Schimpf für Sieg!
Muss ich denn fallen,
nicht fahr' ich nach Walhall —
Hella halte mich fest!

Brünnhilde
(erschüttert).

So wenig achtest du
ewige Wonne?
Alles wär' dir
das arme Weib,
das müd' und harmvoll
matt auf dem Schosse dir hängt?
Nichts sonst hieltest du hehr?

Siegmund
(bitter zu ihr aufblickend).

So jung und schön
erschimmerst du mir:
doch wie kalt und hart
kennt dich mein Herz! —
Kannst du nur höhnen,
so hebe dich fort,
du arge, fühllose Maid!
Doch musst du dich weiden
an meinem Weh',
mein Leid letze dich denn;
meine Noth labe
dein neidvolles Herz: —
nur von Walhall's spröden Wonnen
sprich du wahrlich mir nicht!

Brünnhilde
(mit wachsender Ergriffenheit).

Ich sehe die Noth,
die das Herz dir nagt;
ich fühle des Helden
heiligen Harm — —
Siegmund, befiehl mir dein Weib;
mein Schutz umfange sie fest!

Siegmund.

Kein andrer als ich
soll die Reine lebend berühren:
verfiel ich dem Tod,
die Betäubte tödt' ich zuvor!

Brynhildr.
Volsung! reckless man!
Hark to my rede!
assign me thy bride
for the sake of the babe
to be born of your love-passion sweet.

Siegmund
(drawing his sword).

This sword,
which a traitor for true man designed —
this sword,
which falsely in fight shall betray —
fails it to slaughter my foe,
more fatal 'twill prove to my friend! —
(Holding the sword over *Sieglinda*.)
Two lives here
lie before thee: —
take them, Needful,
terrible steel!
Take them with one fell stroke!

Brynhildr
(quite carried away by sympathy).

Forbear, Volsung!
list to my voice!
Sieglind' shall live still
and Siegmund leave not her side!
'Tis so ordained,
the death-lot cancelled:
thou, Siegmund,
doubt not, safely shalt speed!
(Horn-calls are heard in the distance at back.)
Mark'st thou that horn?
Now hold thyself manned!
Take up thy sword
and swing it with trust:
'twill surely prevail,
for the Valkyrie tenders aid! —
Farewell, Siegmund,
stalwartest man!
at the combat seek for my coming!

She rushes away and disappears with her horse in a defile at side R. *Siegmund* looks after her, joyfully relieved.

The stage has gradually darkened: heavy thunder-clouds gather over the background and cover the rocks, the gorge and the raised peak gradually. — From all sides calls from distant signal-horns are heard, gradually approaching during the following.

Siegmund
(bending over *Sieglinda*).

Slumber's charm
has soothed my fair one's
wild and frenzied woe. —
Did the Valkyrie's heedful care
this quiet divine o'er her cast?

Brünnhilde.
Wälsung! Rasender!
Hör' meinen Rath:
befiehl mir dein Weib
um des Pfandes willen,
das wonnig von dir es empfing!

Siegmund
(sein Schwert ziehend).

Diess Schwert —
das dem Treuen ein Trugvoller schuf;
diess Schwert —
das feig vor dem Feind mich verräth: —
frommt es nicht gegen den Feind,
so fromm' es denn wider den Freund! —
(Das Schwert auf *Sieglinde* zückend.)
Zwei Leben
lachen dir hier: —
nimm sie, Nothung,
neidischer Stahl!
nimm sie mit einem Streich!

Brünnhilde
(im heftigsten Sturme des Mitgefühls).

Halt' ein, Wälsung!
höre mein Wort!
Sieglinde lebe —
und Siegmund lebe mit ihr!
Beschlossen ist's;
das Schlachtloss wend' ich:
dir, Siegmund,
schaff' ich Segen und Sieg!
(Man hört aus dem fernen Hintergrunde Hornrüfe erschallen.)
Du hörst den Ruf?
Nun rüste dich, Held!
Traue dem Schwert
und schwing' es getrost:
treu hält dir die Wehr,
wie die Walküre treu dich schützt! —
Leb' wohl, Siegmund,
seligster Held!
Auf der Walstatt grüss' ich dich wieder!

Sie stürmt fort, und verschwindet mit dem Rosse rechts in einer Seitenschlucht. *Siegmund* blickt ihr freudig und erhoben nach.
Die Bühne hat sich allmälig verfinstert; schwere Gewitterwolken senken sich auf den Hintergrund herab, und hüllen die Gebirgswände, die Schlucht und das erhöhte Bergjoch, nach und nach gänzlich ein. — Von allen Seiten lassen sich aus der Ferne Rüfe von Heerhörnern vernehmen, die während des Folgenden allmälig näher erschallen.

Siegmund
(über *Sieglinde* sich beugend).

Zauberfest
bezähmt ein Schlaf
der Holden Schmerz und Harm: —
da die Walküre zu mir trat,
schuf sie ihr den wonnigen Trost?

Would not the tidings of war
her womanly terrors awake? —
Lifeless she seems
but yet she lives:
her dread is allayed
by loveliest dreams. —
(Renewed horn-calls.)
So slumber in peace,
till the strife is o'er
and peril shall be past.
(He lays her gently on the stone-seat, kisses her forehead, and then, after repeated horn-calls, leaves her.)
The coming foe
firmly must stand;
what he demands
mine to give:
Needful deals him his due.
(He hastens to the back and disappears immediately in the black mists on the mountain peak.)

Sieglinda
(dreaming).

Hies not my father yet home?
Still he hunts with the boy in the forest.
Mother! Mother!
I tremble much!
these strangers' stern looks
terribly strike me! —
Turbid vapours
towering vast —
fiery tongues
are twining around —
they burn the house —
oh help me, brother!
Siegmund! Siegmund!
(Vivid lightning breaks through the clouds; a fearful thunder-clap awakes *Sieglinda*: she starts up suddenly.)
Siegmund! — Ah!

She stares around her with increasing terror: — almost the whole of the stage is hidden in black thunder-clouds; continual thunder and lightning. From all sides come approaching horn-calls.

Hunding's
(voice, at back, from the peak).

Woeful! Woeful!
Stand to the strife!
Say, with my hounds must I hunt thee?

Siegmund's
(voice, further off, in the ravine).

Where hidest thou
that I behold thee not?
Forth, that I may face thee!

Sieglinda
(listening in fearful agitation).

Hunding — Siegmund —
could I but see them!

Sollte die grimmige Wahl
nicht schrecken ein gramvolles Weib? —
Leblos scheint sie,
die dennoch lebt:
der Traurigen kos't
ein lächelnder Traum. —
(Neue Hornrüfe.)
So schlumm're nun fort,
bis die Schlacht gekämpft,
und Friede dich erfreu'!
(Er legt sie sanft auf den Steinsitz, küsst ihr die Stirn, und bricht dann, nach abermaligen Hornrüfen, auf.)
Der dort mich ruft,
rüste sich nun;
was ihm gebührt,
biet' ich ihm:
Nothung zahl' ihm den Zoll!
(Er eilt dem Hintergrunde zu, und verschwindet auf dem Joche sogleich in finstres Gewittergewölk.)

Sieglinde
(träumend).

Kehrte der Vater nun heim!
Mit dem Knaben noch weilt er im Forst.
Mutter! Mutter!
mir bangt der Muth: —
nicht freund und friedlich
scheinen die Fremden! —
Schwarze Dämpfe —
schwüles Gedünst —
feurige Lohe
leckt schon nach uns —
es brennt das Haus —
zu Hülfe, Bruder!
Siegmund! Siegmund!
(Starke Blitze zucken durch das Gewölk auf; ein furchtbarer Donnerschlag erweckt *Sieglinde*: sie springt jäh auf.)
Siegmund! — Ha!

Sie starrt mit steigender Angst um sich her: — fast die ganze Bühne ist in schwarze Gewitterwolken verhüllt; fortwährender Blitz und Donner. Von allen Seiten dringen immer näher Hornrüfe her.

Hunding's
(Stimme, im Hintergrunde vom Bergjoche her).

Wehwalt! Wehwalt!
Steh' mir zum Streit,
sollen dich Hunde nicht halten!

Siegmund's
(Stimme, von weiter hinten her, aus der Schlucht).

Wo birg'st du dich,
dass ich vorbei dir schoss?
Steh' dort, dass ich dich stelle!

Sieglinde
(die in furchtbarer Aufregung lauscht).

Hunding — Siegmund —
könnt' ich sie sehen!

Hunding's
(voice).

Prepare, thou fugitive foeman.
Fricka fates thee my prey!

Siegmund's
(voice, now also on the rocky peak).

Thou weenest me weaponless,
  foolish wight!
Prate not of females,
  but fight unsuccoured;
her minion Fricka forsakes!
For see! from thy house-tree's
  harbouring stem
I drew undaunted this sword;
of its sharpness soon shalt thou judge!

A lightning flash for a moment lights up the crag, on which Hunding and Siegmund are seen fighting.

Sieglinda
(with her utmost strength).

Stay your hands, ye madmen!
  murder first me!

She rushes towards the mountain peak: but so violent a flash of lightning breaks from R. over the combatants, suddenly dazzling her, that she staggers back blinded. In the light-glare appears Brynhildr, soaring over Siegmund and covering him with her shield.

Brynhildr's
(voice).

Fell him, Siegmund!
firm be thy sooth-sword!

Just as Siegmund aims a deadly stroke at Hunding a ruddy glare of light breaks through the clouds, in which appears Wotan, standing over Hunding, and holding his spear defensively against Siegmund.

Wotan's
(voice).

Recoil from my spear!
Be splintered the sword!

Brynhildr retreats in terror with her shield before Wotan: Siegmund's sword snaps on the outstretched spear; Hunding buries his sword in the defenceless man's breast. Siegmund falls to the ground. — Sieglinda, who has heard his death-sigh, sinks down with a cry, as if lifeless.

With Siegmund's fall the glare of light on both sides has faded; dense gloom reigns in the clouds up to the front: through it Brynhildr is indistinctly seen hurrying towards Sieglinda.

Brynhildr.

To horse, that I may help thee!

She lifts Sieglinda quickly with her on to her horse which stands in the defile close by and immediately disappears with her completely.

At this moment the clouds part in the midst and show clearly Hunding withdrawing his sword from the fallen Siegmund. — Wotan, surrounded by clouds, stands behind him on a rock, leaning on his spear and sorrowfully gazing on Siegmund's body.

Hunding's
(Stimme).

Hieher, du frevelnder Freier:
Fricka fälle dich hier!

Siegmund's
(Stimme, nun ebenfalls auf dem Bergjoche).

Noch wähnst du mich waffenlos,
  feiger Wicht?
Droh'st du mit Frauen,
  so ficht nun selber,
sonst lässt dich Fricka im Stich!
Denn sieh': deines Hauses
  heimischem Stamm
entzog ich zaglos das Schwert;
seine Schneide schmecke du jetzt!

Ein Blitz erhellt für einen Augenblick das Bergjoch, auf welchem jetzt Hunding und Siegmund kämpfend gewahrt werden.

Sieglinde
(mit höchster Kraft).

Haltet ein, ihr Männer!
mordet erst mich!

Sie stürzt auf das Bergjoch zu: ein, von rechts her über die Kämpfer ausbrechender, heller Schein blendet sie aber plötzlich so heftig, dass sie wie erblindet zur Seite schwankt. In dem Lichtglanze erscheint Brünnhilde über Siegmund schwebend und diesen mit dem Schilde deckend.

Brünnhilde's
(Stimme).

Triff' ihn, Siegmund!
traue dem Siegschwert!

Als Siegmund soeben zu einem tödtlichen Streiche auf Hunding ausholt, bricht von links her ein glühend röthlicher Schein durch das Gewölk aus, in welchem Wotan erscheint, über Hunding stehend, und seinen Speer Siegmund quer entgegenhaltend.

Wotan's
(Stimme).

Zurück vor dem Speer!
In Stücken das Schwert!

Brünnhilde weicht vor Wotan mit dem Schilde erschrocken zurückgewichen: Siegmund's Schwert zerspringt an dem vorgestreckten Speere; dem Unbewehrten stösst Hunding sein Schwert in die Brust. Siegmund stürzt zu Boden. — Sieglinde, die seinen Todesseufzer gehört, sinkt mit einem Schrei wie leblos zusammen.

Mit Siegmund's Fall ist zugleich von beiden Seiten der glänzende Schein verschwunden; dichte Finsterniss ruht im Gewölk bis nach vorn: in ihm wird Brünnhilde undeutlich sichtbar, wie sie in jäher Hast Sieglinden sich zugewendet.

Brünnhilde.

Zu Ross, dass ich dich rette!

Sie hebt Sieglinde schnell zu sich auf ihr, der Seitenschlucht nahe stehendes Ross, und verschwindet sogleich gänzlich mit ihr.

Alsbald zertheilt sich das Gewölk in der Mitte, so dass man deutlich Hunding gewahrt, wie er sein Schwert dem gefallenen Siegmund aus der Brust zieht. — Wotan, von Gewölk umgeben, steht hinter ihm auf einem Felsen, an seinen Speer gelehnt, und schmerzlich auf Siegmund's Leiche blickend.

Wotan
(after a short silence, turning to *Hunding*).

Get hence, knave!
kneel before Fricka:
tell her how Wotan's spear
avenged his spouse's slight. —
Go! — Go! —

(Before the contemptuous wave of his hand *Hunding* sinks dead to the ground.)

Wotan
(suddenly bursting out in terrible wrath).

But Brynhildr —
vengeance shall break on her!
Fell scourging
shall follow her crime
if my steed may stay her in flight!

(He disappears in thunder and lightning. — The curtain quickly falls.)

THIRD ACT.

On the summit of a rocky mountain.

The stage is bordered R. by a pine-wood. L. the entrance to a cave, forming a natural hall: above this the rock rises to its highest. At back the view is quite open: high and low rocks border a precipice, which is supposed to descend abruptly at back. — Occasional clouds fly past the mountain summit, as if driven by a storm.

(The names of the *eight Valkyries* who, besides *Brynhildr*, take part in this scene, are: *Gerhilda, Ortlinda, Valtrauta, Svertleita, Helmviga, Siegruna, Grimgerda* and *Rossvisa*.)

Gerhilda, Ortlinda, Valtrauta and *Svertleita* are ensconced on the rocky peak above the cave: they are in full armour.

Gerhilda
(higher placed than the rest, calls towards the back).

Hoyotoho! Hoyotoho!
Heiaha! Heiaha!
Helmviga, hail!
Hie here with thy horse!

A flash of lightning breaks through a passing cloud: a Valkyrie on horseback is visible in it; over her saddle hangs a slain warrior.

Helmviga's
(voice from without).

Hoyotoho! Hoyotoho!

Ortlinda, *Valtrauta* und *Svertleita*
(hailing the new-comer).

Heiaha! Heiaha!

(The cloud with the apparition disappears R. behind the wood.)

Ortlinda.
(calling towards the wood).

By Ortlinda's filly
fasten thy horse:

Wotan
(nach einem kleinen Schweigen, zu *Hunding* gewandt).

Geh' hin, Knecht!
Kniee vor Fricka:
meld' ihr, dass Wotan's Speer
gerächt, was Spott ihr schuf. —
Geh'! — Geh'! —

(Vor seinem verächtlichen Handwink sinkt *Hunding* todt zu Boden.)

Wotan
(plötzlich in furchtbarer Wuth auffahrend).

Doch Brünnhilde —
weh' der Verbrecherin:
Furchtbar sei
die Freche gestraft,
erreicht mein Ross ihre Flucht!

(Er verschwindet mit Blitz und Donner. — Der Vorhang fällt schnell.)

DRITTER AUFZUG.

Auf dem Gipfel eines Felsberges.

Rechts begrenzt ein Tannenwald die Scene. Links der Eingang einer Felshöhle, die einen natürlichen Saal bildet: darüber steigt der Fels zu seiner höchsten Spitze auf. Nach hinten ist die Aussicht gänzlich frei; höhere und niedere Felssteine bilden den Rand vor dem Abhange, der — wie anzunehmen ist — nach dem Hintergrunde zu steil hinabführt. — Einzelne Wolkenzüge jagen, wie vom Sturm getrieben, am Felsensaume vorbei.

(Die Namen der *acht Walküren*, welche — ausser *Brünnhilde* — in dieser Scene auftreten, sind: *Gerhilde, Ortlinde, Waltraute, Schwertleite, Helmwige, Siegrune, Grimgerde, Rossweisse*.)

Gerhilde, Ortlinde, Waltraute und *Schwertleite* haben sich auf der Felsspitze, an und über der Höhle, gelagert; sie sind in voller Waffenrüstung.

Gerhilde
(zu höchst gelagert, und dem Hintergrunde zugewendet).

Hojotoho! Hojotoho!
Heiaha! Heiaha!
Helmwige, hier!
Hieher dein Ross!

In einem vorbeiziehenden Gewölk bricht Blitzesglanz aus: *eine Walküre* zu Ross wird in ihm sichtbar: über ihrem Sattel hängt ein erschlagener Krieger.

Helmwige's
(Stimme, von aussen).

Hojotoho! Hojotoho!

Ortlinde, *Waltraute* und *Schwertleite*
(der Ankommenden entgegenrufend).

Hejaha! Hejaha!

(Die Wolke mit der Erscheinung ist rechts hinter dem Tann verschwunden.)

Ortlinde
(in den Tann hineinrufend).

Zu Ortlinde's Stute
stell' deinen Hengst:

gladly my grey
will graze near thy chestnut!

Valtrauta
(the same).

Who hangs at thy saddle?

Helmviga
(entering from the pine wood).

Sintolt the Hegeling.

Svertleita.

Fasten thy chestnut
far from the grey then:
Ortlinda's mare
carries Vittig the Irming!

Gerhilda
(descending somewhat lower).

As foes I have seen them,
Sintolt and Vittig.

Ortlinda
(starting up and running into the wood).

Heiaha! Thy mare
is mauled by my horse.

Svertleite and *Gerhilda*
(laughing aloud).

The heroes' strife
lives still in the horses.

Helmviga
(calling back towards the wood).

Hey there, Brownie!
Break not the concord.

Valtrauta
(who has assumed the look-out on the peak instead of *Gerhilda*).

Hoyotoho! Hoyotoho!
Heiaha! Heiaha!
Siegruna, here!
Where stay'st thou so long?

(*Siegruna* flies past in the air towards the wood in the same manner as *Helmviga*.)

Siegruna's
(voice from R).

Occupied!
Are the others all here?

The Valkyries.

Hoyotoho! Hoyotoho!
Heiaha! Heiaha!

(*Siegruna* disappears behind the wood. From below are heard two voices together.)

Grimgerda and *Rossvisa*
(from below).

Hoyotoho! Hoyotoho!
Heiaha! Heiaha!

mit meiner Grauen
gras't gern dein Brauner!

Waltraute
(ebenso).

Wer hängt dir im Sattel?

Helmwige
(aus dem Tann schreitend).

Sintolt der Hegeling!

Schwertleite.

Führ' deinen Braunen
fort von der Grauen:
Ortlinde's Mähre
trägt Wittig den Irming!

Gerhilde
(ist etwas näher herabgestiegen).

Als Feinde sah ich nur
Sintolt und Wittig.

Ortlinde
(bricht schnell auf, und läuft in den Tann).

Heiaha! Die Stute
stösst mir der Hengst!

Schwertleite und *Gerhilde*
(lachen laut auf).

Die Rosse entzweit noch
der Recken Zwist!

Helmwige
(in den Tann zurückrufend).

Ruhig dort, Brauner!
Brichst du den Frieden?

Waltraute
(hat für *Gerhilde* die Wacht auf der äussersten Spitze genommen).

Hojotoho! Hojotoho!
Heiaha! Heiaha!
Siegrune, hier!
Wo säumst du so lang?

(Wie zuvor *Helmwige*, zieht jezt *Siegrune* im gleichen Aufzuge vorbei, dem Tann zu.)

Siegrune's
(Stimme von rechts).

Arbeit gabs!
Sind die And'ren schon da?

Die Walküren.

Hojotoho! Hojotoho!
Heiaha! Heiaha!

(*Siegrune* ist hinter dem Tann verschwunden. Aus der Tiefe hört man zwei Stimmen zugleich.)

Grimmgerde und *Rossweisse*
(von unten).

Hojotoho! Hojotoho!
Heiaha! Heiaha!

Valtrauta.	*Waltraute.*
Grimgerd' and Rossvisa!	Grimgerd' und Rossweisse!
Gerhilda.	*Gerhilde.*
Arriving at once.	Sie reiten zu zwei.
Ortlinda has returned from the wood with *Helmviga* and the newly arrived *Siegruna:* all three signal from the edge of the precipice towards the depth.	Ortlinde ist mit *Helmwige* und der so eben angekommenen *Siegrune* aus dem Tann herausgetreten: zu drei winken sie von dem hinteren Felssaume hinab.
Ortlinda, Helmviga and *Siegruna.*	*Ortlinde, Helmwige* und *Siegrune.*
We greet ye, riders twain! Rossvis' and Grimgerda!	Gegrüsst, ihr Reissige! Rossweiss' und Grimgerde!
All the other Valkyries.	*Die andren Walküren alle.*
Hoyotoho! Hoyotoho! Heiaha! Heiaha!	Hojotoho! Hojotoho! Heiaha! Heiaha!
In a lightning-illumined cloudbank, which rises from the valley and then disappears behind the wood, appear *Grimgerda* and *Rossvisa*, also on horseback and bearing slain warriors.	In einem blitz-erglänzenden Wolkenzuge, der von unten her aufsteigt und dann hinter dem Tann verschwindet, erscheinen *Grimgerde* und *Rossweisse*, ebenfalls auf Rossen, jede einen Erschlagenen im Sattel führend.
Gerhilda.	*Gerhilde.*
Your steeds in the forest let stand and feed!	In Wald mit den Rossen zu Weid' und Rast!
Ortlinda (calling into the wood).	*Ortlinde* (in den Tann rufend).
Fasten the mares afar from each other, till all our heroes' hate be allayed!	Führt die Mähren fern von einander, bis uns'rer Helden Hass sich gelegt!
Gerhilda (whilst all the others laugh).	*Gerhilde* (während die Andren lachen).
The grey, in sooth, through their feud has suffered.	Der Helden Grimm schon büsste die Graue!
(*Grimgerda* and *Rossvisa* enter from the wood.)	(*Grimgerde* und *Rossweisse* treten aus dem Tann auf.)
The Valkyries.	*Die Walküren.*
Be welcome! Be welcome!	Willkommen! Willkommen!
Svertleita.	*Schwertleite.*
Went ye wanderers paired?	War't ihr Kühnen zu zwei?
Grimgerda.	*Grimgerde.*
Alone journeyed we, but lately we met.	Getrennt ritten wir, trafen uns heut'.
Rossvisa.	*Rossweisse.*
Stand we fully assembled? then stay no longer: to Valhall' wend we our way, victims for Wotan provide.	Sind wir alle versammelt, dann säumt nicht lange: nach Walhall brechen wir auf, Wotan zu bringen die Wal.
Helmviga.	*Helmwige.*
Are there but eight? All are not here.	Acht sind wir erst: eine noch fehlt.

Gerhilda.
By the brawny Volsung
Valorous Brynhild'.

Valtrauta.
For her arrival
must we still rest:
Wotan would give us
greeting full grim,
should he not see her with us!

Siegruna.
(from the rocky peak where she is looking out).
Hoyotoho! Hoyotoho!
Behold! Behold!
In breath-devoid haste
flies Brynhildr here.

The Valkyries
(hastening towards the rock).
Heiaha! Heiaha!
Brynhildr! Hey!

Valtrauta.
To the wood she guides
her wavering horse.

Grimgerda.
How snorts Grani
from swift career!

Rossvisa.
I saw never thus
a Valkyrie speeding!

Ortlinda.
What mounts she in saddle?

Helmviga.
That is no man!

Siegruna.
'Tis a maid merely.

Gerhilda.
Where met she that maid?

Svertleita.
Without a hail
she hies toward us!

Valtrauta.
Heiaha! Brynhildr!
Hearest thou not?

Gerhilde.
Bei dem braunen Wälsung
weilt wohl noch Brünnhild'.

Waltraute.
Auf sie noch harren
müssen wir hier:
Walvater gäb' uns
grimmigen Gruss,
säh' ohne sie er uns nah'n!

Siegrune
(auf der Felsspitze, von wo sie hinausspäht).
Hojotoho! Hojotoho!
Hieher! Hieher!
In brünstigem Ritt
jagt Brünnhilde her.

Die Walküren
(nach der Felsspitze eilend).
Heiaha! Heiaha!
Brünnhilde! hei!

Waltraute.
Nach dem Tann lenkt sie
das taumelnde Ross.

Grimgerde.
Wie schnaubt Grane
vom schnellen Ritt!

Rossweisse.
So jach sah ich nie
Walküren jagen!

Ortlinde.
Was hält sie im Sattel?

Helmwige.
Das ist kein Held!

Siegrune.
Eine Frau führt sie.

Gerhilde.
Wie fand sie die Frau?

Schwertleite.
Mit keinem Gruss
grüsst sie die Schwestern?

Waltraute.
Heiaha! Brünnhilde!
hörst du uns nicht?

Ortlinda.
Help our sister
to earth in safety.
(*Gerhilda* and *Helmwiga* rush into the wood.)

Rossvisa.
To ground hath sunk
Grani the stalwart!
(*Siegruna* and *Valtrauta* follow the other two.)

Grimgerda.
From the saddle lifts she
lightly the maid.

The other Valkyries
(hastening towards the wood).
Sister! Sister!
What is thy strait!
the Valkyries re-enter; with them comes *Brynhildr* supporting and leading *Sieglinda*.)

Brynhildr.
(breathlessly).
Shield me — O help
in hardest need!

The Valkyries.
Why fliest thou here
in furious haste?
So flee but culprits who fear!

Brynhildr.
I am for the first time
pursued in flight!
Host-Father hunts me down!

The Valkyries
(in sudden terror).
Wander thy senses?
Say! speak to us!
Doth follow Host-Father?
Fleest thou from him?

Brynhildr
(anxiously).
O sisters, scale ye
the mountain's summit!
Spy to northward,
if Wotan draws nigh.
(*Ortlinda* and *Valtrauta* spring up to the look-out.)
Speak! shews he in sight?

Ortlinda.
A thunder-gale
nears from northward.

Valtrauta.
Gathering thick
groweth the cloud.

Ortlinde.
Helft der Schwester
vom Ross sich schwingen!
(*Gerhilde* und *Helmwige* stürzen in den Tann.)

Rossweisse.
Zu Grunde stürzt
Grane der starke!
(*Siegrune* und *Waltraute* folgen den beiden.)

Grimgerde.
Aus dem Sattel hebt sie
hastig das Weib.

Die übrigen Walküren
(dem Tann zueilend).
Schwester! Schwester!
Was ist gescheh'n?
(*Alle Walküren* kehren auf die Bühne zurück: mit ihnen kommt *Brünnhilde*, *Sieglinde* unterstützend und hereingeleitend.)

Brünnhilde
(athemlos).
Schützt mich, und helft
in höchster Noth!

Die Walküren.
Wo rittest du her
in rasender Hast?
So fliegt nur wer auf der Flucht!

Brünnhilde.
Zum erstenmal flieh' ich
und bin verfolgt!
Heervater hetzt mir nach!

Die Walküren
(heftig erschreckend).
Bist du von Sinnen?
Sprich! Sage uns!
Verfolgt dich Heervater?
fliehst du vor ihm?

Brünnhilde
(ängstlich).
O Schwestern, späht
von des Felsens Spitze!
Schaut nach Norden,
ob Walvater naht!
(*Ortlinde* und *Waltraute* springen hinauf, um zu spähen.)
Schnell! seht ihr ihn schon?

Ortlinde.
Gewittersturm
naht von Norden.

Waltraute.
Starkes Gewölk
staut sich dort auf.

The Valkyries.

Host-Father strideth
his heavenly steed.

Brynhildr.

The savage hunter
pursuing in haste,
he nears, he nears from northward!
Shield me, sisters!
Watch o'er this woman!

The Valkyries.

Who is she, this woman?

Brynhildr.

Brief be my answer —
Sieglinda is she,
Siegmund's sister and bride:
Wotan with virulence
vows the Volsungs to waste: —
The brother should
by Brynhild's help
to-day have been slain.
I sheltered Siegmund,
though, with my shield,
slighting the god,
who slew him himself with his spear.
Siegmund fell
and I fled
far with his friend:
to preserve her
hither I hied
to beseech your help
In staving off the blow from us both.

The Valkyries
(in great consternation).

Unworthy sister!
What words are these?
Woe's me! Woe's me!
Brynhildr! woe's thee!
Brok'st thou with daring,
Brynhildr,
Host-Father's holiest ban?

Valtrauta
(from the height).

Nears the tempest
like night from the north.

Ortlinda
(the same).

Raging storm-clouds
hitherward stride.

Die Walküren.

Heervater reitet
sein heiliges Ross!

Brünnhilde.

Der wilde Jäger,
der wüthend mich jagt,
er naht, er naht von Nord!
Schützt mich, Schwestern!
wahret dies Weib!

Die Walküren.

Was ist mit dem Weibe?

Brünnhilde.

Hört mich in Eile!
Sieglinde ist es,
Siegmund's Schwester und Braut:
gegen die Wälsungen
wüthet Wotan in Grimm: —
dem Bruder sollte
Brünnhilde heut'
entziehen den Sieg:
doch Siegmund schützt' ich
mit meinem Schild,
trotzend dem Gott: —
der traf ihn da selbst mit dem Speer.
Siegmund fiel:
doch ich floh
fern mit der Frau:
sie zu retten
eilt' ich zu euch,
ob mich bange auch
ihr berget vor dem strafenden Streich.

Die Walküren
(in grösster Bestürzung).

Bethörte Schwester!
Was thatest du?
Wehe! Wehe!
Brünnhilde, wehe!
Ungehorsam
brach Brünnhilde
Heervaters heilig Gebot?

Waltraute
(von der Höhe).

Nächtig ziehet es
von Norden heran.

Ortlinde
(ebenso).

Wüthend steuert
hieher der Sturm.

DIE WALKUERE.

The Valkyries
(turning towards the back).
Howls herald
Host-Father's steed:
shrilly snorting it flies!

Brynhildr.
Woe to the victim,
if Wotan should strike!
To wailing and death
devotes he the Volsungs! —
Who'll lend me a horse,
the lightest of foot,
to whirl this woman away?

The Valkyries.
Shall we likewise
learn to defy?

Brynhildr.
Rossvisa — sister!
Lend me thy racer!

Rossvisa.
He never yet fled
our father in fear.

Brynhildr.
Helmviga, hear me!

Helmviga.
Our father I hold to.

Brynhildr.
Grimgerda! Gerhilda!
Grant me a horse!
Svertleita! Siegruna!
See my distress!
Be still my friends —
O fall not away!
Save this unfortunate wife!

Sieglinda
(who has hitherto gazed gloomily and blankly before her, starts as *Brynhildr* suddenly clasps her protectingly).
O suffer no sorrow for me!
Ah! how dear now were death!
Who bade thee, maid,
to bear me from peril?
A stroke I might
in the strife have found
from the self-same weapon
that Siegmund fell by:
then had I fallen
and hied with him.
Far from Siegmund —
Siegmund, from thee!

Die Walküren
(dem Hintergrunde zugewendet).
Wild wiehert
Walvaters Ross,
schrecklich schnaubt es daher!

Brünnhilde.
Wehe der Armen,
wenn Wotan sie trifft,
den Wälsungen allen
droht er Verderben! —
Wer leih't mir von euch
das leichteste Ross,
das flink die Frau ihm entführ'?

Die Walküren.
Auch uns räth'st du
rasenden Trotz?

Brünnhilde.
Rossweise, Schwester!
Leih' mir deinen Renner!

Rossweisse.
For Walvater floh
der fliegende nie.

Brünnhilde.
Helmwige, höre!

Helmwige.
Dem Vater gehorch' ich.

Brünnhilde.
Waltraute! Gerhilde!
Gönnt mir eu'r Ross!
Ortlinde! Siegrune!
Seht meine Angst!
O seid mir treu,
wie traut ich euch war:
rettet diess traurige Weib!

Sieglinde
(die bisher finster und kalt vor sich hingestarrt, fährt auf, als *Brünnhilde* sie lebhaft — wie zum Schutze — umfasst).
Nicht sehre dich Sorge um mich ·
einzig taugt mir der Tod!
Wer hiess dich Maid
dem Harst mich entführen?
Im Sturm dort hätt' ich
den Streich empfah'n
von derselben Waffe,
der Siegmund fiel:
das Ende fand ich
vereint mit ihm!
Fern von Siegmund —
Siegmund, von dir!

O'ermaster, oh death!
my sad remembrance!
If thou wouldst court not,
maiden, my curses,
then one pray'r in pity accord me —
strike with thy sword to my heart.

Brynhildr.
Live still, oh wife,
for the love that waits thee!
Rescue the pledge
that with thee he hath placed:
a very Volsung thou bearest!

Sieglinda
(is violently startled: suddenly her features light up with sublime joy).
Rescue me, brave one!
rescue my babe!
Shelter me, maidens,
with mightiest shield!

(A fearful thunderstorm rises at back: approaching thunder.)

Valtrauta
(from the peak).
The storm gathers fast.

Ortlinda
(the same).
Fly, all who fear it!

The Valkyries.
Hence with the woman,
wrath threatens her:
the Valkyries may not
venture to aid!

Sieglinda
(kneeling to *Brynhildr*).
Save me, oh maid!
Spurn not a mother!

Brynhildr
(with sudden determination).
Then fly with all swiftness —
and fly by thyself!
I'll — stay where I am;
strike on me Wotan's anger:
while I hinder him
here in his wrath,
thou by flight shalt escape from his curse.

Sieglinda.
Where may I safely wander?

Brynhildr.
Which of ye, sisters,
sped to the eastward?

O deckte mich Tod,
dass ich's nicht denke! —
Soll um die Flucht
dir Maid ich nicht fluchen,
so erhöre heilig mein Fleh'n —
stosse dein Schwert mir in's Herz!

Brünnhilde.
Lebe, o Weib,
um der Liebe willen!
Rette das Pfand,
das von ihm du empfing'st:
ein Wälsung wächst dir im Schosse!

Sieglinde.
(ist heftig erschrocken: plötzlich strahlt dann ihr Gesicht in erhabener Freude auf).
Rette mich, Kühne!
rette mein Kind!
Schirmt mich, ihr Mädchen,
mit mächtigstem Schutz!

(Furchtbares Gewitter steigt im Hintergrunde auf: nahender Donner.)

Waltraute
(von der Höhe).
Der Sturm kommt heran.

Ortlinde
(ebenso).
Flieh' wer ihn fürchtet!

Die Walküren.
Fort mit dem Weibe,
droht ihm Gefahr:
der Walküren keine
wag' ihren Schutz!

Sieglinde
(auf den Knieen vor *Brünnhilde*).
Rette mich,
rette die Mutter!

Brünnhilde
(mit schnellem Entschluss).
So fliehe denn eilig —
und fliehe allein!
Ich — bleibe zurück,
biete mich Wotan's Rache:
an mir zögr' ich
den Zürnenden hier,
während du seinem Rasen entrinnst.

Sieglinde.
Wohin soll ich mich wenden?

Brünnhilde.
Wer von euch Schwestern
schweifte nach Osten?

DIE WALKUERE.

Siegruna.
To east a tangled
forest extends:
the Nibelung's hoard
has Fafnir fled there to hide.

Svertleita.
Changed to a dread
dragon the churl is;
and in a hole
he harbours with Alberic's ring.

Grimgerda.
'Tis no haven there
for a helpless wife.

Brynhildr.
And yet from Wotan's wrath
shelter sure were this wood:
'tis shunned by him:
he abhorreth the spot.

Valtrauta
(on the height).
Raging rides
the god to our rock.

The Valkyries.
Brynhild', hark
to the gathering bruit!

Brynhildr
(pointing out the direction to *Sieglinda*).
Fly then swiftly,
and speed to the east!
Bravely determine
all trials to bear—
hunger and thirst,
thorns and hard ways;
smile through all pain
while suffering pangs!
This only heed
and hold it ever:
the highest hero of worlds
hid'st thou, oh wife,
in sheltering shrine!—
(She gives her the pieces of *Siegmund's* sword.)
For him keep these shreds
of shattered sword-blade;
from his father's death-field
by fortune I saved them:
anon renewed,
this sword shall he swing,
and now his name I declare—
"Siegfried"—victory's son!

Siegrune.
Nach Osten weithin
dehnt sich ein Wald:
der Niblungen Hort
entführte Fafner dorthin.

Schwertleite.
Wurmes-Gestalt
schuf sich der Wilde:
in einer Höhle
hütet er Alberich's Reif.

Grimgerde.
Nicht geheu'r ist's dort
für ein hülflos Weib.

Brünnhilde.
Und doch vor Wotan's Wuth
schützt sie sicher der Wald:
ihn scheut der Mächt'ge
und meidet den Ort.

Waltraute
(von der Höhe).
Furchtbar fährt
dort Wotan zum Fels.

Die Walküren.
Brünnhilde, hör'
seines Nahen's Gebraus'!

Brünnhilde
(*Sieglinden* die Richtung weisend).
Fort denn, eile
nach Osten gewandt!
Muthigen Trotzes
ertrag' alle Müh'n—
Hunger und Durst,
Dorn und Gestein;
lache, ob Noth
und Leiden dich nagt!
Denn eines wisse
und wahr' es immer:
den hehrsten Helden der Welt
hegst du, o Weib,
im schirmenden Schoss!—
(Sie reicht ihr die Stücken von Siegmund's Schwert.)
Verwahr' ihm die starken
Schwertes-Stücken;
seines Vaters Walstatt
entführt' ich sie glücklich:
der neu gefügt
das Schwert einst schwingt,
den Namen nehm' er von mir—
„Siegfried" freu' sich des Sieg's!

Sieglinda.
O marvellous sayings!
maiden divine!
What comfort o'er
my mind thou hast cast!
For his sake I live
and save this belov'd one:
may my blessing frame
future reward!
Fare thee well!
Be Sieglind's sorrow thy weal!

(She hastens off R. in the foreground. — The rocky heights are veiled in black thunder-clouds; a fearful storm rages up from the back: a fiery glow illumines the pine-wood at side. Between the peals of thunder *Wotan's* voice is heard.

Wotan's.
(voice).
Stay, Brynhildr!

The Valkyries.
Now steed and rider
reach the rocks here:
woe, Brynhildr!
wrath doth he bring!

Brynhildr.
Ah, sisters, help!
I sink at heart!
His ire will crush me
if from my aid ye recoil.

The Valkyries.
Then here, thou lost one,
lest thou be seen!
Shelter in our midst:
be silent when called.

(They all gather on the rocky peak, while *Brynhildr* hides in their midst.)

Woe! ah, woe's thee!
wildly springeth
Wotan from horse —
hither hurls
in haste for revenge!

Wotan.
Wotan strides on from the pine-wood in terrible angry emotion and halts before the crowd of *Valkyries*, who have so placed themselves on the height as to conceal *Brynhildr.*

Where is Brynhildr?
where the rebellious one?
Dare ye to veil her
from Wotan's vengeance?

The Valkyries.
Fearful and dread thy dictate: —
what did, oh father, thy daughters,
that such a storm
they have stirred in thy breast?

Sieglinde.
Du hehrstes Wunder!
herrliche Maid!
Dir Treuen dank' ich
heiligen Trost!
Für ihn, den wir liebten,
rett' ich das Liebste:
meines Dankes Lohn
lache dir einst!
Lebe wohl!
Dich segnet Sieglinde's Weh'!

Sie eilt rechts im Vordergrunde ab. — Die Felsenhöhe ist von schwarzen Gewitterwolken umlagert; furchtbarer Sturm braus't aus dem Hintergrunde daher: ein feuriger Schein erhellt den Tannenwald zur Seite. Zwischen dem Donner hört man *Wotan's* Ruf.

Wotan's
(Stimme).
Steh'! Brünnhilde!

Die Walküren.
Den Fels erreichten
Ross und Reiter:
weh' dir, Brünnhilde!
Rache entbrennt!

Brünnhilde.
Ach, Schwestern, helft!
mir schwankt das Herz!
Sein Rorn zerschellt mich,
wenn eu'r Schutz ihn nicht zähmt.

Die Walküren.
Hieher, Verlor'ne!
lass' dich nicht seh'n!
Schmiege dich an uns,
und schweige dem Ruf!

(Sie ziehen sich alle die Felsspitze hinauf, indem sie *Brünnhilde* unter sich verbergen.)

Wehe! Wehe!
Wüthend schwingt sich
Wotan vom Ross —
hieher ras't
sein rächender Schritt!

Wotan.
Wotan schreitet in furchtbar zürnender Aufregung aus dem Tann heraus, und hält vor dem Haufen der *Walküren* an, die auf der Höhe eine Stellung einnehmen, durch welche sie *Brünnhilde* schützen.

Wo ist Brünnhilde?
wo die Verbrecherin?
Wagt ihr, die Böse
vor mir zu bergen?

Die Walküren.
Schrecklich ertos't dein Toben: —
was thaten, Vater, die Töchter,
dass sie dich reizten
zu rasender Wuth?

Wotan. Would ye defy me? Foolish ones, tremble! I know Brynhildr hides here from me. Hence from her aid! the outcast from heaven, who all things high has spurned from her! *The Valkyries.* To us sped the pursued one, for our said seeking with pray'rs! She sees thy rage in silence and ruth. For our truant sister trembling we sue, that thy fury's burst may abate. *Wotan.* Weak-spirited, womanish brood! Such melting moods ye won not from me! I tempered your frames for fighting and toil, steeled, too, your bosoms to bear distress, and you minions now moan and groan when I grimly chastise breach of faith? No wist ye, waverers, what she hath wrought for whom your tremulous tear-drops arise! No one like she knew what my bosom enshrouded! not one like she spied to the depths of my spirit: 'twas she worked what my will had shaped and designed:— and now is broken our notable bond when, faith-annulling, my will she defied, my sacred command openly scorned, against me attempting to turn e'en the tools by me bestowed! — Hear'st thou, Brynhildr? Thou on whom byrnie, helm and glaive, glory and hope, honour and strength I bestowed? How to my chiding canst harken, and fail to face the chider, in hope from thy doom to hide?	*Wotan.* Wollt ihr mich höhnen? Hütet euch, Freche! Ich weiss: Brünnhilde bergt ihr vor mir. Weichet von ihr, der ewig Verworf'nen, wie ihren Werth von sich sie warf! *Die Walküren.* Zu uns floh die Verfolgte, unsren Schutz flehte sie an! mit Furcht und Zagen fasst sie dein Zorn. Für die bange Schwester bitten wir nun, dass den ersten Zorn du bezähm'st. *Wotan.* Weichherziges Weibergezücht! So matten Muth gewannt ihr von mir? Erzog ich euch kühn zu Kämpfen zu zieh'n, schuf ich die Herzen euch hart und scharf, dass ihr Wilden nun weint und greint, wenn mein Grimm eine Treulose straft? So wisst denn, Winselnde, was die verbrach, um die euch Zagen die Zähre entbrennt! Keine wie sie kannte mein innerstes Sinnen! keine wie sie wusste den Quell meines Willens; sie selbst war meines Wunsches schaffender Schoss: — und so nun brach sie den seligen Bund, dass treulos sie meinem Willen getrotzt, mein herrschend Gebot offen verhöhnt, gegen mich selbst die Waffe gewandt, die allein mein Wunsch ihr schuf! — Hörst du's Brünnhilde? du, der ich Brünne, Helm und Wehr, Wonne und Huld, Namen und Leben verlieh? Hörst du mich Klage erheben, und birgst dich bang dem Kläger, dass feig du der Straf' entflöh'st?

THE VALKYRIE.

Brnyhildr
(steps out from the group of *Valkyries*, descends with downcast mien, but firm tread, from the rock and advances thus to within a short distance from *Wotan*.)
Hear stand I, father:
to suffer my sentence!

Wotan.
I — sentence thee not:
thou hast shaped the stroke for thyself.
Thy father's will
awoke thee to life,
yet against that will thou hast warr'd:
acting my orders
was only thy part
yet against me all hast thou ordered:
Wish-maid
wert to me,
yet against me now hast thou wished:
Shield-maid
wert to me,
yet against me turnedst thy shield:
Lot-chooser
thou wert to me,
yet against me lot hast thou chosen:
Hero-stirrer
thou wert to me,
yet against me stirrest thou heroes.
What wert thou erst
Wotan hath uttered:
what now thou art
that say for thyself!
Wish-maid art thou no more;
one time a Valkyrie wert thou —
remain henceforth
but merely thyself.

Brynhildr
(in sudden terror).
Thou disownest me?
Thine aim I divine!

Wotan.
From Valhall ne'er more will I send thee;
I'll cause thee no more
warriors to call;
no more bring'st thou heroes
to fill my hall;
at the Æsir's festal meeting
the flagon no more
thou'llt fill me with mead;
ne'er shall I kiss more
thy sweet, childlike mouth.
From heavenly clans
are thou excluded,
bann'd, degraded
from thy blessed degree;
for broken now are all bonds:
exiled for aye, are thou banished from bliss.

Brünnhilde.
(tritt aus der Schaar der *Walküren* hervor, schreitet demüthigen, doch festen Schrittes von der Felsenspitze herab, und tritt so in geringer Entfernung vor Wotan).
Hier bin ich Vater:
gebiete die Strafe!

Wotan.
Nicht — straf' ich dich erst:
deine Strafe schuf'st du dir selbst.
Durch meinen Willen
war'st du allein:
gegen ihn doch hast du gewollt;
meinen Befehl nur
führtest du aus:
gegen ihn doch hast du befohlen;
Wunsch-Maid
war'st du mir:
gegen mich doch hast du gewünscht;
Schild-Maid
war'st du mir:
gegen mich doch hob'st du den Schild;
Loos-Kieserin
war'st du mir:
gegen mich doch kies'test du Loose;
Helden-Reizerin
war'st du mir:
gegen mich doch reiztest du Helden.
Was sonst du war'st,
das sagte dir Wotan:
was jetzt du bist,
das sage dir selbst!
Wunschmaid bist du nicht mehr;
Walküre bist du gewesen: —
nun sei fortan,
was so du noch bist!

Brünnhilde
(heftig erschrocken.)
Du verstössest mich?
versteh' ich den Sinn?

Wotan
Nicht send' ich dich mehr aus Walhall,
nicht weis' ich dir mehr
Helden zur Wal;
nicht führ'st du mehr Sieger
in meinen Saal:
bei der Götter traulichem Mahle
das Trinkhorn reich'st du
mir traut nicht mehr;
nicht kos' ich dir mehr
den kindischen Mund.
Von göttlicher Schaar
bist du geschieden,
ausgestossen
aus der Ewigen Stamm;
gebrochen ist unser Bund:
aus meinem Angesicht bist du verbannt.

The Valkyries
(breaking into lamentation).
Horror! Woe!
Sister! Oh Sister!

Brynhildr.
All thou hast given
again wouldst take?

Wotan.
To thy lord all must thou lose!
And here, where we stand
strikes thee my curse;
in powerless sleep
shalt thou be cast:
that man shall seize on the maid
in whose way she is seen and awaked.

The Valkyries.
Oh stay, recall it!
recall thy curse!
Shall the maiden wither
and waste by a man?
Thou grim father, deal not
this grievous disgrace:
as her sisters we share in her shame!

Wotan.
Did ye not hear
what I ordained?
From your resort
must the treacherous sister be severed;
no more a-horse [tempest;
with your troop will she hurl through the
her maidenhood's flower
will fade unmarked;
a consort will claim her
in conjugal clasp:
she'll follow her master
henceforth at his beck,
by fire to sit and to spin,
to free spirits a mock and sport.

(Brynhildr sinks wailing upon the ground at his feet; the Valkyries make a movement of terror.)

Fear ye her doom?
Then fly the condemned one.
Draw from her side
and hold ye afar!
Dares one unduteous
near her to dally,
dares one defy me
and furnish her help —
that fool shall find a like fate:
so, bold ones, I bid ye heed! —
Make no more halt!
seek not this mountain!

Die Walküren.
(in Jammer ausbrechend).
Wehe! Wehe!
Schwester! O Schwester!

Brünnhilde.
Nimmst du mir alles,
was einst du gab'st?

Wotan.
Der dich zwingt, wird dir's entzieh'n!
Hieher auf den Berg
banne ich dich;
in wehrlosen Schlaf
schliesse ich dich;
der Mann dann fange die Maid,
der am Wege sie findet und weckt.

Die Walküren.
Halt' ein, Vater!
halt' ein mit dem Fluch!
Soll die Maid verblüh'n
und verbleichen dem Mann?
Du Schrecklicher, wende
die schreiende Schmach:
wie die Schwester träf' uns ihr Schimpf!

Wotan.
Hörtet ihr nicht,
was ich verhängt?
Aus eurer Schaar
ist die treulose Schwester geschieden;
mit euch zu Ross
durch die Lüfte nicht reitet sie länger;
die magdliche Blume
verblüht der Maid;
ein Gatte gewinnt
ihre weibliche Gunst:
dem herrischen Manne
gehorcht sie fortan,
am Herde sitzt sie und spinnt,
aller Spottendeu Ziel und Spiel.

(Brünnhilde sinkt schreiend vor seinen Füssen zu Boden; die Walküren machen eine Bewegung des Entsetzens.)

Schreckt euch ihr Loos?
So flieht die Verlor'ne!
Weichet von ihr
und haltet euch fern!
Wer von euch wagte
bei ihr zu weilen,
wer mir zum Trotz
zu der Traurigen hielt' —
die Thörin theilte ihr Loos:
das künd' ich der Kühnen an!
Fort jetzt von hier!
meidet den Felsen!

Hence I warn ye to hasten,
lest I hurl woe on your heads.

The *Valkyries* separate with a wild cry of woe and seek hasty flight into the wood, whence they are presently heard to whirl away on their horses through the storm. — Gradually, during the following scene, the thunderstorm abates; the clouds disperse: evening twilight and finally night, fall with tranquil weather.

Wotan and *Brynhildr*, she still prostrate at his feet, remain alone. — Long solemn silence: *Wotan* and *Brynhildr* preserve their positions.

Brynhildr

(at last slowly raising her head, seeks *Wotan's* averted gaze, and during the following gradually rises to her feet).

Was it so shameful
what I have done,
that for my deed I so shamefully am scourged?
Was it so base
to warp thy command,
that thou to me such debasement must shape?
Was't such dishonour
what I have wrought,
that it should rob me of honour for aye?
O speak, father!
see me before thee!
Soften thy wrath,
wreak not thine ire,
but make to me clear
the mortal guilt
that with cruel firmness compels thee
to cast off thy favourite child!

Wotan
(gloomily).

Ask of thy deed —
'twill surely shew thee thy guilt.

Brynhildr.

But thy decree
I carried out.

Wotan.

Decreed I then
care of Volsung in combat?

Brynhildr.

Thou toldest me so
to turn the event.

Wotan.

But I revoked
my unavailing behest.

Brynhildr.

When Fricka thine own
intending did frustrate; —
when *her* intending was followed
to thyself wert thou false.

Hurtig jagt mir von dannen,
sonst erharrt Jammer euch hier!

Die *Walküren* fahren mit wildem Wehschrei auseinander und stürzen in hastiger Flucht in den Tann: bald hört man sie wie mit Sturm auf ihren Rossen davonjagend. — Nach und nach legt sich während des Folgenden das Gewitter; die Wolken verziehen sich: Abenddämmerung, und endlich Nacht, sinken bei ruhigem Wetter herein.

Wotan und *Brünnhilde*, die noch zu seinen Füssen hingestreckt liegt, sind allein zurückgeblieben. — Langes, feierliches Schweigen: unveränderte Stellung *Wotan's* und *Brünnhilde's*.

Brünnhilde

(endlich das Haupt langsam erhebend, sucht *Wotan's* noch abgewandten Blick, und richtet sich während des Folgenden allmälig ganz auf).

War es so schmählich,
was ich verbrach, [straf'st?
War es so niedrig,
was ich dir that,
dass du so tief mir Erniedrigung schaff'st?
War es so ehrlos,
was ich beging,
dass mein Vergeh'n nun die Ehre mir raubt?
O sag', Vater!
sieh' mir in's Auge:
schweige den Zorn,
zähme die Wuth!
Deute mir hell
die dunkle Schuld,
die mit starrem Trotze dich zwingt
zu verstossen dein trautestes Kind!

Wotan
(finster).

Frag' deine That —
sie deutet dir deine Schuld!

Brünnhilde.

Deinen Befehl
führte ich aus.

Wotan.

Befahl ich dir
für den Wälsung zu fechten?

Brünnhilde.

So hiessest du mich
als Herrscher der Wal.

Wotan.

Doch meine Weisung
nahm ich wieder zurück.

Brünnhilde.

Als Fricka den eig'nen
Sinn dir entfremdet:
da ihrem Sinn du dich fügtest,
warst du selber dir Feind.

Wotan
(bitterly).

I knew thou understoodst my meaning,
and scourge now thy mutinous act;
though weak and dull
dost thou think me:
but that I must trample out treason,
thou wert truly too mean for my wrath.

Brynhildr.

My wisdom's scanty;
I wist though of one thing—
that thou well lov'dst the Volsung:
I wist of thy struggle,
thy constraint
to hide that love in oblivion.
Thou only held'st
that other decree—
though the shameful hap
shadowed thy heart—
that Siegmund should not be shielded.

Wotan.

And deeming it so
thou daredst to lend him thy shield?

Brynhildr.

'Twas because I held
in my heart thy true wish,
which, by covenants hampered,
fatally clogged,
now thou renouncest so weakly.
I who follow Wotan
and fare in his wake,
have seen a thing once
by thee unseen:
Siegmund straight I sought.
I hied
to him with his fate,
I looked on his features,
heard him at large;
I was stirred by the hero's
holy distress;
widely resounded
the warrior's sorrow —
free was his passion,
fearful his pain,—
mournfullest courage,
confident might;
and my ear did list,
and my eyes did look on,
what bade in fulness my heart
with holy fervour to beat. —
Shy, astonished
stood I ashamed;

Wotan
(bitter).

Dass du mich verstanden, wähnt' ich,
und strafte den wissenden Trotz;
doch feig und dumm
dachtest du mich:
so hätt' ich Verrath nicht zu rächen,
zu gering wär'st du meinem Grimm?

Brünnhilde.

Nicht weise bin ich;
doch wusst' ich das Eine —
dass den Wälsung du liebtest:
ich wusste den Zwiespalt,
der dich zwang,
diess Eine ganz zu vergessen,
Das Andre musstest
einzig du seh'n,
was zu schauen so herb
schmerzte dein Herz —
dass Schutz du Siegmund versagtest.

Wotan.

Du wusstest es so,
und wagtest dennoch den Schutz?

Brünnhilde.

Weil für dich im Auge
das Eine ich hielt,
dem, im Zwange des Andren
schmerzlich entzweit,
rathlos den Rücken du wandtest.
Die im Kampfe Wotan
den Rücken bewacht,
die sah nun Das nur,
was du nicht sah'st: —
Siegmund musste ich seh'n.
Tod kündend
trat ich vor ihn,
gewahrte sein Auge,
hörte sein Wort;
ich vernahm des Helden
heilige Noth;
tönend erklang mir
des Tapfersten Klage —
freiester Liebe
furchtbares Leid,
traurigsten Muthes
mächtigster Trotz:
meinem Ohr erscholl,
mein Aug' erschaute,
was tief im Busen das Herz
zu heil'gem Beben mir traf. —
Scheu und staunend
stand ich in Scham:

I could consider
but how to serve him:
safety or shame
with Siegmund to share them—
this was the fiat
I fain had decreed!
Thou who this love
within my heart hid,
whose purpose had placed
me at his side,
firm, faithful to thee—
thwarted I thy command.

Wotan.
Thou didst for me
what I wished so dearly to work,
but was forced to leave;
by fate doubly induced.
With ease ween'st thou
owin then the heart's fondest wishes?
When burning woe
in my heart I bore,
when rankling distress
my rage awoke,
that while deeply loving,
my love untold
in my tortured heart must be hidden:—
when 'gainst my own self
I in suff'ring contended,
and from my spleen
of spirit in wrath sprang,
wasted with longings,
languished with woe,
the furious wish did I form
in the wreck of my tottering world
these eternal wrestlings to termine:—
yet lapp'd wert thou
in thralling delights;
blissful emotion's
unrestrained might,
thou drankest lightly
the lovely draught—
while I, god though I be,
bitterest gall-cup must drain!
Thy so light turned soul
let henceforth lead thee:
from me see thyself released!
Thus shall I shun thee,
nor share more with thee
my thoughts and wishes whispered;
apart, ne'er more
in company work we.
So, while life-days shall last,
may the god not give thee his greeting

Brynhildr.
Unfit for thee

ihm nur zu dienen
konnt' ich noch denken:
Sieg oder Tod
mit Siegmund zu theilen —
diess nur erkannt' ich
zu kiesen als Loos!
Der mir in's Herz
diese Liebe gehaucht,
dem Willen, der mich
dem Wälsung gesellt,
ihm innig vertraut —
trotzt' ich deinem Gebot.

Wotan.
So thatest du,
was so gern zu thun ich begehrt —
doch was nicht zu thun
die Noth zwiefach mich zwang?
So leicht wähntest du
Wonne der Liebe erworben,
wo brennend Weh'
in das Herz mir brach,
wo grässliche Noth
den Grimm mir schuf,
einer Welt zu Liebe
der Liebe Quell
im gequälten Herzen zu hemmen?
Wo gegen mich selbst
ich sehrend mich wandte,
aus Ohnmacht-Schmerzen
schäumend ich aufschoss,
wüthender Sehnsucht
sengender Wunsch
den schrecklichen Willen mir schuf,
in den Trümmern der eig'nen Welt
meine ewige Trauer zu enden:—
da labte süss
dich selige Lust;
wonniger Rührung
üppigen Rausch
enttrankst du lachend
der Liebe Trank—
als mir göttlicher Noth
nagende Galle gemischt?
Deinen leichten Sinn
lass' dich denn leiten:
du sagtest von mir dich los!
Dich muss ich meiden,
gemeinsam mit dir
nicht darf ich Rath mehr raunen;
getrennt nicht dürfen
traut wir mehr schaffen:
so weit Leben und Luft,
darf der Gott dir nicht mehr begegnen!

Brünnhilde.
Wohl taugte dir nicht

was the foolish maid
who, stunned by thy counsel,
nought understood,
while her own conviction
but one thing advised —
to love all that thou didst love. —
If we must sever
ourselves for ever,
if thou tearest
what once was intact,
the one half putting
far from thy presence —
that once was girt to thy service,
thou god, forget not this! —
Thine own estate
thou dar'st not dishonour;
seek not so deeply
to shame thyself;
thyself would then be sullied,
seeing me scoffed at and scorned.

Wotan.

Thou fain hast followed
the might of love:
follow now him
whom thou must needs love!

Brynhildr.

Shall I from Valhall sever,
no more to thy service be vassal,
my life to a mortal
belong from henceforth?
To boasting poltroon
give not the prize:
by a worthless churl
let me not be won.

Wotan.

From Fate-father hast thou turned:
Thy fate no more may he move.

Brynhildr.

Once mad'st thou a glorious breed;
no mean one shall ever debase it:
one valiant o'er all — I vouch it —
shall spring from Volsung's line.

Wotan.

Peace, with thy Volsung's line!
As thou'rt relinquished,
lost too is that:
'twas wrecked by me in my wrath.

Brynhildr.

I, who crossed thee so,
saved it from doom:
Sieglinda holds

die thör'ge Maid,
die staunend im Rathe
nicht dich verstand,
wie mein eig'ner Rath
nur das Eine mir rieth —
zu lieben was du geliebt. —
Muss ich denn scheiden
und scheu dich meiden,
musst du spalten
was einst sich umspannt,
die eig'ne Hälfte
fern von dir halten —
dass sonst sie ganz dir gehörte,
du Gott, vergiss das nicht!
Dein ewig Theil
nicht wirst du entehren,
Schande nicht wollen,
die dich beschimpft;
dich selbst liessest du sinken,
säh'st du dem Spott mich zum Spiel!

Wotan.

Du folgtest selig
der Liebe Macht:
folge nun dem,
den du lieben musst!

Brünnhilde.

Soll ich aus Walhall scheiden,
mit dir nicht mehr schaffen und walten;
soll ich gehorchen
dem herrschenden Mann —
dem feigen Prahler
gieb mich nicht preis!
nicht werthlos sei er,
der mich gewinnt.

Wotan.

Von Walvater schiedest du —
nicht wählen darf er für dich.

Brünnhilde.

Du zeugtest ein edles Geschlecht;
kein Zager kann ihm entschlagen:
der weihlichste Held — ich weiss es —
entblüht dem Wälsungenstamm.

Wotan.

Schweig' von dem Wälsungenstamm!
Von dir geschieden
schied ich von ihm:
vernichten musst' ihn der Neid.

Brünnhilde.

Die von dir sich riss —
ich rettete ihn:
Sieglinde hegt

the holiest fruit;
in anguish sore
such as woman ne'er suffered
will she give birth
to the babe she bears.

Wotan.

Ne'er seek at my hand
safety to find
even for her sireless fruit!

Brynhildr.

She guardeth the sword
thou hast shaped for Siegmund. —

Wotan.

And which I into splinters struck. —
Seek not, oh maid,
for means to unnerve me!
Bemoan not thy fate,
move as it may:
I cannot cast thee the lot! —
But hence must I fare,
hasten away;
too long I'm wavering here.
Now I turn from thee
as thou didst from me;
I would know nought
of what thou dost wish:
thy punishment
I must promptly deal.

Brynhildr.

What hast thou designed
that I must suffer?

Wotan.

Unbreaking sleep
shall seal thy sense:
what man the wardless maid wakes,
that wight shall win her to wife.

Brynhildr
(falling on her knees).

Shall fetters of sleep
firmly bind me,
to fall a booty
to any braggart?
This one thing must thou allow me:
forlorn, I urge thee to hear!
My helpless form hedge round
with hindering horrors,
that but by a free man,
fearless of heart,
here on the fell
I may be found!

die heiligste Frucht;
in Schmerz und Leid,
wie kein Weib sie litt,
wird sie gebären
was bang sie birgt.

Wotan.

Nie suche bei mir
Schutz für die Frau,
noch für ihres Schosses Frucht!

Brünnhilde.

Sie bewahrt das Schwert,
das du Siegmund schuf'st. —

Wotan.

Und das ich in Stücken ihm schlug. —
Nicht streb', o Maid,
den Muth mir zu stören!
Erwarte dein Loos,
wie sich's dir wirft:
nicht kiesen kann ich es dir! —
Doch fort muss ich jetzt,
fern von dir zieh'n:
zuviel schon zögert' ich hier,
Von der Abwendigen
wend' ich mich ab;
nicht wissen darf ich
was sie sich wünscht:
die Strafe nur
muss vollstreckt ich seh'n.

Brünnhilde.

Was hast du erdacht
dass ich erdulde?

Wotan.

In festen Schlaf
verschliess' ich dich:
wer so die Wehrlose weckt,
dem ward, erwacht, sie zum Weib.

Brünnhilde
(stürzt auf ihre Knie).

Soll fesselnder Schlaf
fest mich binden,
dem feigsten Manne
zur leichten Beute:
diess Eine musst du erhören,
was heil'ge Angst zu dir fleht!
Die Schlafende schütze
mit scheuchenden Schrecken:
dass nur ein furchtlos
freiester Held
hier auf dem Felsen
einst mich fänd'!

Wotan.

Too much thou beggest —
the boon's too great!

Brynhildr
(clinging to his knees).

This one thing must
thou concede me!
O chasten thy child,
who enchains thy knees;
down-tread the true heart,
destroy thou thy maid;
let her vital spark
be sped by thy spear;
but cast, cruel one, ne'er
such crushing disgrace as this!
(Wildly).
At thy command
let magical fire
spring forth and enfold me,
lambent and fierce,
to lick with its tongue,
to rend with its teeth
the trembler who rashly dareth
to ravish the rock of its prize.

Wotan
(gazes into her eyes with emotion and raises her up).

Farewell, my brave
and beautiful child!
Thou once the life
and light of my heart,
farewell, farewell, farewell!
Loth I must leave thee;
no more in love
may I grant thee my greeting;
henceforth my maid
ne'er more with me rideth,
nor waiteth wine to reach me.
When I relinquish
thee, my belov'd one,
thou laughing delight of my eyes,
thy bed shall be lit
by torches more brilliant
than ever for bridal have burned!
Fiery gleams
shall girdle the fell,
with terrible scorching
scaring the timid,
who, cowed, may cross not
Brynhildr's couch: —
for one alone free-eth the bride;
one freer than I, the god!

(*Brynhildr*, touched and enraptured, throws herself into his arms.)

Wotan.

Zu viel begehrst du —
der Gunst zu viel!

Brünnhilde
(seine Knie umfassend).

Diess Eine musst —
musst du erhören!
Zerknicke dein Kind,
das dein Knie umfasst;
zertritt die Traute,
zertrümm're die Maid;
ihres Leibes Spur
zerstöre dein Speer:
doch gieb, Grausamer, nicht
der grässlichsten Schmach sie preis!
(Mit Wildheit.)
Auf dein Gebot
entbrenne ein Feuer;
den Fels umglühe
lodernde Gluth:
es leck' ihre Zunge
und fresse ihr Zahn
den Zagen, der frech es wagte
dem freislichen Felsen zu nah'n!

Wotan
(blickt ihr ergriffen in das Auge, und hebt sie auf).

Leb' wohl, du kühnes
herrliches Kind!
Du meines Herzens
heiliger Stolz,
leb' wohl! leb' wohl! leb' wohl!
Muss ich dich meiden,
und darf minnig
mein Gruss nimmer dich grüssen;
sollst du nicht mehr
neben mir reiten,
noch Meth beim Mahl mir reichen;
muss ich verlieren
dich, die ich liebte,
du lachende Lust meines Auges: —
ein bräutliches Feuer
soll dir nun brennen,
wie nie einer Braut es gebrannt!
Flammende Gluth
umglühe den Fels;
mit zehrenden Schrecken
scheuch' es den Zagen,
der Feige fliehe
Brünnhilde's Fels: —
denn Einer nur freie die Braut,
der freier als ich, der Gott!

Brünnhilde wirft sich ihm gerührt und entzückt in die Arme.

THE VALKYRIE.

Wotan.

These eyes so lustrous and clear,
which oft in love I have kissed,
 when warlike longings
 won my lauding,
 or when with lispings
 of heroes leal
thy honied lips were inspired; —
these effulgent, glorious eyes,
whose flash my gloom oft dispelled,
 when hopeless cravings
 my heart discouraged,
 or when my wishes
 toward worldly pleasure
from wild warfare were turning: —
 their lustrous gaze
 lights on me now
 as my lips imprint
 this last farewell!
On happier mortal
here shall they beam;
the grief-suffering god
may never henceforth behold them!
 Now, heart-torn,
 he gives thee his kiss
and taketh thy god-hood away.

He kisses her on both eyes, which then remain closed: she sinks gently unconscious back in his arms. He bears her tenderly and lays her on a low mossy mound over-shadowed by a wide spreading fir-tree. Again he gazes on her features, then closes her helmet vizor; once more his look rests sorrowfully on her form, which he at last covers with the long steel shield of the Valkyrie. — Then he stalks with solemn resolution to the middle of the stage and turns the point of his spear towards a huge rocky boulder.

Loki, hear!
listen and heed!
As I found thee at first,
 a fiery glow,
as thou fleddest me headlong,
 a hovering glimmer,
as then I bound thee,
 bound be thou now!
Appear, wavering spirit,
and spread me thy fire round this fell!
Loki! Loki! appear!

At the last invocation he strikes his spear-point thrice against the rock, which thereupon emits a stream of fire: this quickly swells to a sea of flame, which Wotan, with a sign of his spear, directs to encircle the rock.—

He who my spear
 in spirit feareth
ne'er springs through this fiery bar!

(He disappears in the flames at back. — The Curtain falls.)

Wotan.

Der Augen leuchtendes Paar,
das oft ich lächelnd gekos't,
 wenn Kampfes-Lust
 ein Kuss dir lohnte,
 wenn kindisch lallend
 der Helden Lob
von holden Lippen dir floss; —
dieser Augen strahlendes Paar,
das oft im Sturm mir geglänzt,
 wenn Hoffnungs-Sehnen
 das Herz mir sengte,
 nach Welten-Wonne
 mein Wunsch verlangte
aus wild bebendem Bangen: —
 zum letzten Mal
 letz' es mich heut'
 mit des Lebewohles
 letztem Kuss!
Dem glücklicher'n Manne
glänze sein Stern;
dem unseligen Ew'gen
muss es scheidend sich schliessen!
 Denn so — kehrt
 der Gott sich dir ab:
so küsst er die Gottheit von dir.

*Er küsst sie auf beide Augen, die ihr sogleich verschlossen bleiben: sie sinkt sanft ermattend in seinen Armen zurück. Er geleitet sie zart auf einen niedrigen Mooshügel zu liegen, über den sich eine breitästige Tanne ausstreckt. Noch einmal betrachtet er ihre Züge, und schliesst ihr dann den Helm fest zu; dann verweilt sein Blick nochmals schmerzlich auf ihrer Gestalt, die er endlich mit dem langen Stahlschilde der Walküre zudeckt. —
Dann schreitet er mit feierlichem Entschlusse in die Mitte der Bühne und kehrt die Spitze seines Speers gegen einen mächtigen Felsstein.*

Loge, hör'!
lausche hieher!
Wie zuerst ich dich fand
 als feurige Gluth,
wie dann einst du mir schwandest
 als schweifende Lohe:
wie ich dich band,
 bann' ich dich heut'!
Herauf, wabernde Lohe,
umlod're mir feurig den Fels!
Loge! Loge! Hieher!

Bei der letzten Anrufung schlägt er mit der Spitze des Speeres dreimal auf den Stein, worauf diesem ein Feuerstrahl entfährt, der schnell zu einem Flammenmeere anschwillt, dem Wotan mit einem Winke seiner Speerspitze den Umkreis des Felsens als Strömung zuweis't. —

Wer meines Speeres
 Spitze fürchtet,
durchschreite das Feuer nie!

(Er verschwindet in der Gluth nach dem Hintergrunde zu. — Der Vorhang fällt.)